# A Priory Revealed

## using material relating to

## Merton Priory

## Cover illustration: A roof boss from Merton priory, discovered during excavations at Nonsuch palace

*The stone the builders rejected has become the capstone*
Luke 20:17

A roof boss is the keystone of the vaulting ribs supporting a groined roof. This example is 4 foot (1.2m) in diameter and weighs 4½ cwt (230kg). The four main rib sections are 1 ft (30cm) square, with four smaller ribs. The purpose of the keystone is to weight the ribs and prevent them from rising or collapsing. Because of the greater length of the diagonal cross rib, the top of the arch was flatter, which required a boss of sufficient breadth to bear on the shaped stones at the top of the curves.

The decoration includes the stems of vine leaves in two rows intertwined. Between the leaves and tendrils are bunches of fruit. The background is coloured red and the leaves and berries gilded. The hole in the centre of a large flower was presumably for hanging a chandelier.

Natural foliage began to appear in decorations about 1250 following conventional trefoil leaves but came to an end by 1320. The introduction of lierne vaulting in 1350 increased the number of bosses required but their quality diminished.

Mark Samuel, formerly stone specialist at MoLAS, has kindly provided further information. The boss is dated to somewhere between 1290 and 1325 on the basis of its mouldings, and is thought to be contemporary with the eastern arm of the priory. The joints were re-cut during repairs in the 1390s.

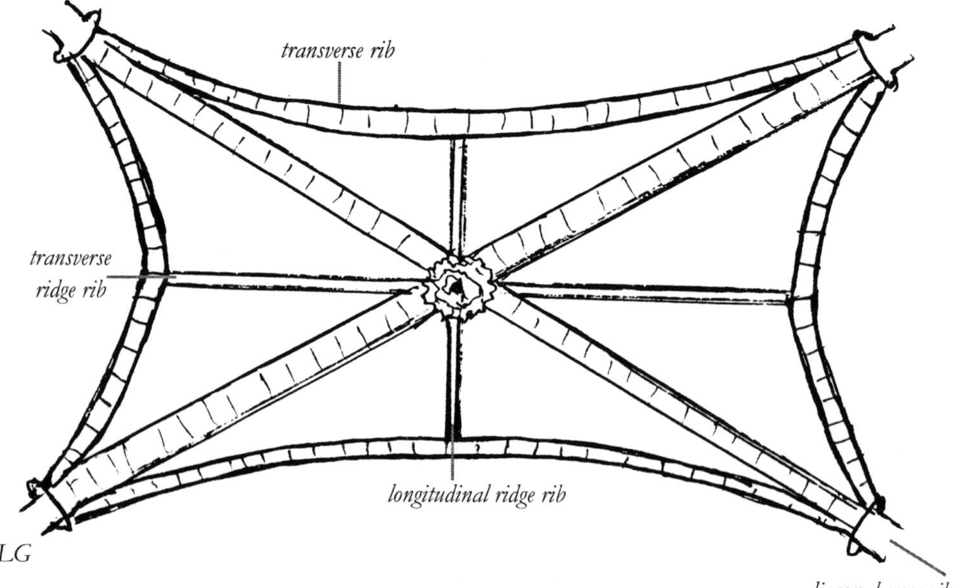


*The cover illustration is reproduced by courtesy of the Museum of London (ref. CL02/8783)*

# A Priory Revealed

## using material relating to

# Merton Priory

LIONEL GREEN

MERTON HISTORICAL SOCIETY
in association with
MERTON PRIORY TRUST

Published by
MERTON HISTORICAL SOCIETY
in association with
MERTON PRIORY TRUST
2005



ISBN 1 903899 52 4

Printed by intypelibra
Units 3/4 Elm Grove Industrial Estate
Elm Grove, Wimbledon SW19 4HE

# CONTENTS

## List of illustrations

## List of Tables

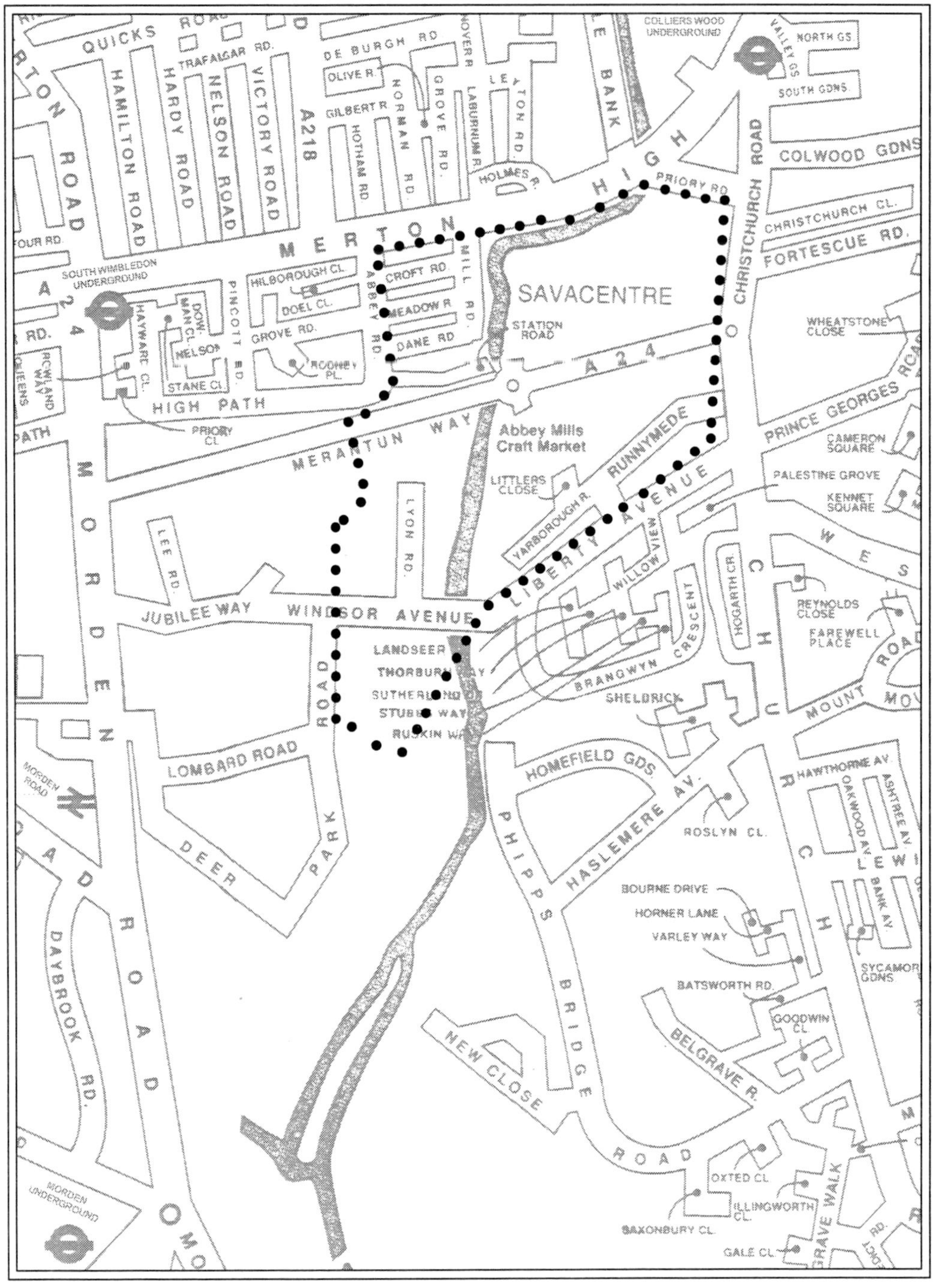


*Detail from a modern street map, with the outline of the priory precinct superimposed (Reproduced by permission of Merton Design Unit, London Borough of Merton)*

# Acknowledgements

The most significant acknowledgement is to Alfred Heales in gratitude and admiration. He compiled *The Records of Merton Priory* at the end of the nineteenth century. His records cover the whole period of the priory's existence and consist of a thousandentries, mostly of the thirteenth century, and form the basis of this book. To produce this outstanding store of information without any errors would have been improbable, and learned critics have revealed embarrassing misdatings, duplications, as well as transcription and translation mistakes. Many of the charters of prior 'E' were ascribed to Eustace (1249-1263), but belong to Egidius or Giles (1222-1263). In the year of publication Heales was suffering a terminal illness and not able to amend any of the misunderstandings.

Another outstanding contribution to the early history of the priory was the transcription and summary of the *Historia Fundationis* by the American scholar, Prof. Marvin Colker, together with his publication on the life of Guy of Merton (d.1124). His kind gift to me of copies of the published work has been of inestimable value.

Thanks must also go to those who have dug to extract information from below ground. These include Col. H F Bidder (1921/2), Dennis Turner (1962/3), Scott McCracken (1976-78, 1983), Penny Bruce and Simon Mason (1986-90) and David Saxby (1992-2001). I am grateful to Dennis, Scott and David for reading, and commenting on, a draft of this book. All plans drawn of the priory in this book have been from small-scale popular plans and are conjectural. We await with patience the publication of the full site report by MoLAS. Meanwhile, I have found useful the two joint publications on the priory by MoLAS and the London Borough of Merton.

It is a pleasure to acknowledge the careful reading and helpful criticism by the editorial committee of the Merton Historical Society (Judith Goodman, Peter Hopkins, Eric Montague and Tony Scott). Their comments have reduced inaccuracies and made the story more readable. I cannot fully express my gratitude to Peter Hopkins (chairman) who encouraged me to complete a task I started long ago. His boundless patience in the preparation for publication over a long period is appreciated. I take full responsibility for any errors which remain.

Acknowledgement is due to many for permission to reproduce illustrations:- M Biddle and Nonsuch Palace Excavation Committee (106), Bodleian Library, Oxford (36), British Library (87), J Goodman (53), P Hopkins (80, 84), London Borough of Sutton (106), J S McCracken (42, 57, 114), Merton Library & Heritage Service (4, 61, 62-3, 116), R Miller (108), MoLAS (20, 44, 53, 57, 64, 96), Museum of London (cover), National Archives (103), W J Rudd (23, 60, 105, 110, back cover), D Saxby (44, 53, 64), Society of Antiquaries (15, 23), Surrey Archaeological Society (7, 57, 71, 100, 114), D Turner (7), Wimbledon Society (9, 61, 62-3). Every effort has been made to trace copyright holders, and I apologise to any who may have been omitted.

Finally, my thanks to Merton Historical Society and Merton Priory Trust for agreeing to publish this book.

Lionel Green. October 2005

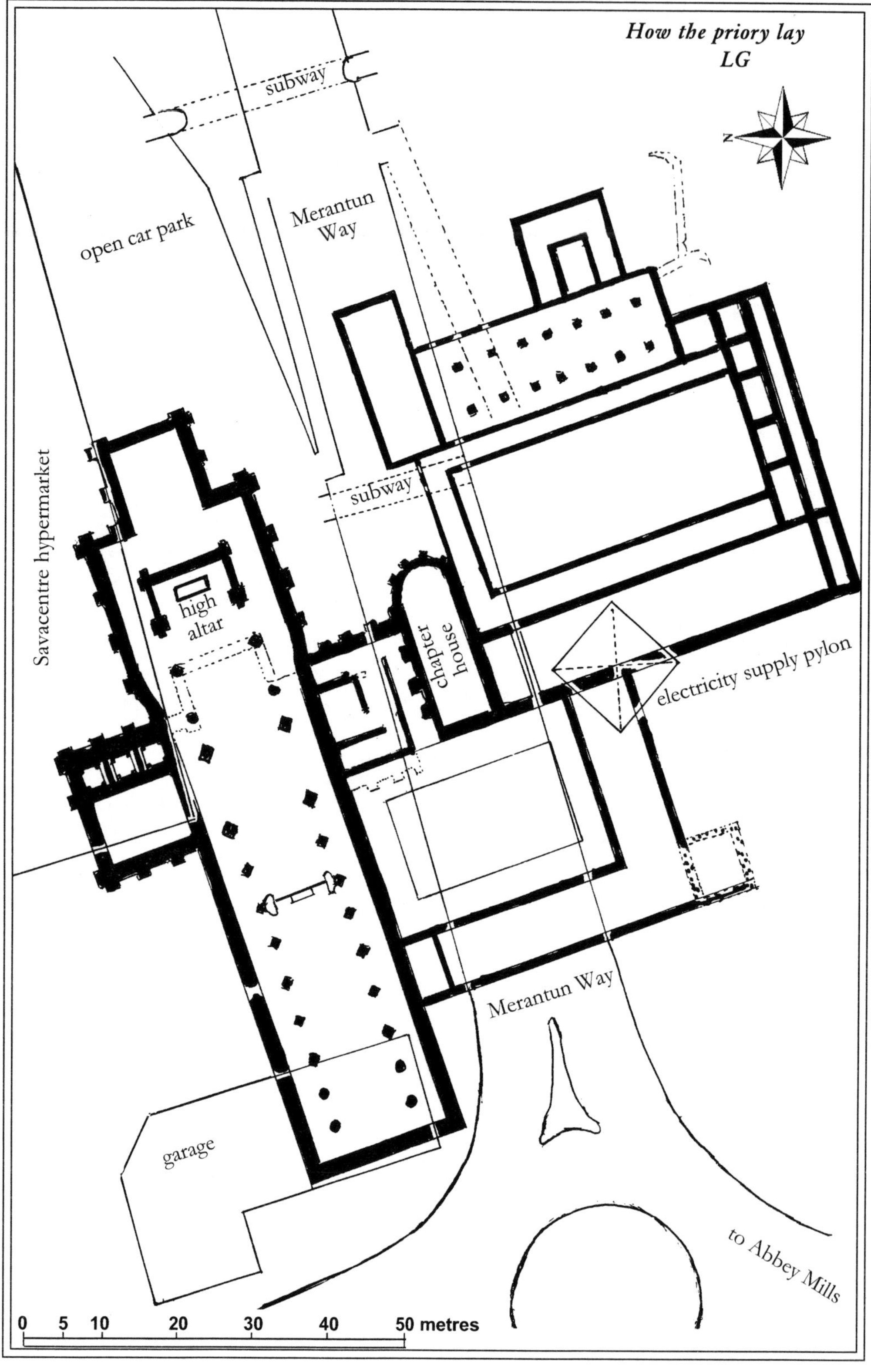
How the priory lay
LG
N
subway
open car park
Merantun Way
Savacentre hypermarket
subway
high altar
chapter house
electricity supply pylon
Merantun Way
garage
to Abbey Mills
0 5 10 20 30 40 50 metres

# Prologue

The year is 1537. Imagine for a moment that in the community is a cathedral-like church which was there in the days of parents, grand-parents and their forebears. This was a monastery which was the centre of activity of almost every family. All had a part to play in a working complex of buildings and farms.

Rumours began to circulate that the monastery was to be closed, and gossip tells of the king wishing to pull down everything. Cardinal Wolsey, with the Pope's blessing, closed 21 understaffed monasteries between 1525 and 1529. This precedent "made all the forest of religious foundations in England to shake, justly fearing that the King would finish to fell the oaks, seeing the cardinal began to cut the underwood".[1]

In July 1531 an Augustinian priory at Aldgate in London was suppressed. It was similar in size and importance to Merton, with a tower housing a ring of nine bells. It was to be demolished and "then was the priory church and steeple proffered to whomsoever would take it down and carry it from the ground, but no man would undertake the offer".[2]

The owner of Aldgate, Sir Thomas Audley, decided to realise the value of the stone, timber, lead, iron etc., and employed his own workmen, who "with great labour, beginning at the top, loosed stone from stone, and threw them down, whereby the most part of them were broken, and few remained whole, and those were sold very cheap for all the buildings then made in the city were of brick and timber. At that time any man in the city might have a cart-load of hard stone for paving brought to his door for 6d or 7d [2½p or 3p] with the carriage".[2]

In March 1537 it was the turn of Lewes priory to be demolished. The work was entrusted to an Italian engineer, Giovanni Portinari, who brought 17 workmen from London. The agent of Thomas Cromwell remarked that "these are men exercised much better than the men that we find here in the country".[3] The agent continues "Now we are plucking down a higher vault borne up by four thick pillars 14ft [4.3m] from side to side and 45 ft [14m] in circumference…and that we brought from London…3 carpenters, 2 smiths, 2 plumbers and one that keepeth the furnace. Everyone of these attendeth to his own office. Ten of them hewed the walls about, among which there were three carpenters; these made props to underset where others cut away, the others broke and cut the walls".[3] This referred to the 32 pillars supporting the roof, which rose to the height of 63 ft (19.2m) from the ground.[4]

The high cost of this operation may have saved other monasteries from complete destruction.

Gothic buildings were easy to demolish. Each arch depended on support of a neighbour. A miner could dig under one of the crossing piers, shoring up with timber as work progressed. A fire lit within the shoring would sink the pier, and all the arches above it would collapse. Adjoining arcades, deprived of their abutment would fall, bringing down the heavy vaults they had safely carried for centuries.[4]

In the spring of 1538 two men rode into Merton to visit the priory. One was Christopher Dickenson, master bricklayer, and the other William Clement, master carpenter. They were on their way from Hampton Court to the king at Greenwich Palace carrying building plans for royal approval. These were for new palaces at Oatlands and Nonsuch, and they called at Merton to assess suitable material to be removed for the king's use at Nonsuch. They went on to the proposed site at Cuddington in order to set out work and confirm requirements.[5]

The Surveyor-General of the King's Works was James Needham, but the works group for Surrey was based at Hampton Court under the control of Richard Benese. He was a leading surveyor and a canon of Merton from before 1530. Whilst at Merton he wrote a book on surveying in 1537, which passed through five editions. He was present in the chapter house on 16 April 1538 and witnessed the surrender of the priory into the king's hands.

Merton was now suppressed, and demolition began immediately. There would have been countless workmen and craftsmen employed at the priory, but would they be willing to destroy the work of their own hands? All strata of society had difficult decisions to make. Principles could so easily be forgotten, especially where there was a family to feed and no prospect of other employment.

Dickenson and Clement, the earlier visitors to the priory, were to supervise the salvage work and the conveyance of materials to Nonsuch,[6] and the building accounts of Nonsuch begin with payments for two clerks on 22 April 1538.[7] Fifty carters were employed from Cheam, Clapham, Cuddington, Malden, Merton, Mitcham, Morden, Putney, Sutton, Tooting, Wandsworth, and Wimbledon. Each received eight pence (3p) for a ton load for the four-mile (6.4km) journey.[8] At first the stone was thrown indiscriminately into carts which travelled as fast as the rough roads would allow. These deliveries, in early May, were mainly of worked stone which went into the foundations of the new palace, being unsuitable for use above ground.[9] This included sculptured heads, fruit and animals.

When the roof of the priory church fell, one of the early 14th-century keystones (bosses) survived the crash almost intact. Despite its weight (4½ cwt, 230 kg) it was hoisted on to a wagon and carted to Nonsuch where it was incorporated into the new palace.

By July 1538, 2,719 tons (2762 tonnes) of stone had been conveyed from Merton. Thereafter the loading decreased, with only 924 tons (938 tonnes) between July and September, suggesting that the bulk of the demolition was completed by July.[10]

Day after day the smoke and dust pervaded the district, visible from the surrounding hills. Tears must have been shed as the villagers of Wimbledon, Morden, Mitcham and Tooting witnessed the collapse of the tower, so familiar as part of the view from Wimbledon and St Mary's church; from Ridgway and Cannon Hill; from Morden and St Lawrence's church; from Pollards Hill; and from Tooting Bec. That which had dominated the view for centuries was no more.

When the tower of Merton fell the bells would have broken into portable pieces for transportation to the foundries, to be cast into cannon for the new coastal castles.

The remains of the priory church thereafter were lost to sight. The land needed time to make it suitable for farming. The sedge withered from the ponds and no birds sang.

It would be another 360 years before Colonel Bidder and his gardener revealed the true size and extent of the priory of Merton. Excavations have continued since the 1920s, mostly in the 1980s and 1990s by the Surrey Archaeological Society and the Museum of London and a full site report will be published shortly by MoLAS. For this reason little archaeological information will be found in these pages.

But what was the priory of Merton? How did it begin? What was its purpose? What did it achieve? What effect did it have on its locality? These are some of the questions this book seeks to answer as the different aspects are examined and the priory is revealed.

*The seal of 1241 as depicted in Brayley's* History of Surrey *Vol III (1882) p.185*

*19th-century drawing of the surviving chapel at Merton 'Abbey' by Richard Simpson (reproduced from the collection of Simpson Papers by courtesy of Merton Library and Heritage Service)*

'Remains of the CHAPEL
at
MERTON ABBEY
SURREY'

# Introduction

Everyone seeks peace. Peace within ourselves – in families – with neighbours – in the world. Early Christian ascetics sought peace with God. They wished to attain a higher spiritual life by retiring to remote spots where they lived as hermits[11] in rigorous self-discipline and a life of unceasing prayer to 'the author of peace and lover of concord'.

In AD 305 St Anthony the anchorite drew together a number of hermits in Egypt to form a community. The idea found its way to Rome, where Christians were living together in the catacombs.[12]

About AD 529 Benedict founded his monastery at Monte Cassino near Naples, and drew up rules of behaviour. When pope Gregory I sent Augustine and his companions to England in 596, they set up a monastery at Canterbury which followed the Rule of St Benedict. Other monasteries were founded in Anglo-Saxon England and all followed the Benedictine Rule. Many became centres of learning and art.

The Norman period brought a new epoch in monasticism. It started in Burgundy after an immense abbey had been founded at Cluny in 909 which had a great influence. Daughter houses were set up, and all followed a more elaborate code of living. In 1077 (or 1081), William de Warenne founded Lewes Abbey with monks from Cluny. Again in Burgundy, several monks of the community of Molesme sensed a fall in standards set by the Benedictine Rule and moved to a new site in 1098, to follow a stricter way of life. The new site was at Cîteaux (Latin - *Cistercium*). But it was to be another 30 years before the first English Cistercian house was founded at Waverley, Surrey, to be followed by Rievaulx and Fountains in Yorkshire.

**The Augustinian Order** takes its name from another St Augustine (d.430), of Hippo, a bishopric on the North African coast (now Bône, Algeria). The Order followed a rule based upon a letter containing spiritual advice for a house of nuns in order to restore concord there in about AD 423.

Like other Orders, the Augustinians observed the seven canonical Hours in church and the vows of obedience, poverty and chastity. This meant obedience to their superior, sharing all things, accepting celibacy and fasting.

Amongst other duties, they gave alms to the needy, provided hospitality to travellers and interceded for the souls of benefactors. It was probably the brevity and vagueness of the rule that marked the success of the Order.

The Order was not an enclosed order, i.e. members could with permission mingle with the outside world. All professed members were priests, and were able to serve parishes and hospitals in their care. They also had a duty to oversee their estates and be self-supporting.

St Augustine held the view that God made an ideal world and man should imitate and reflect this. In the early days of monasticism every action was related to God and linked to Eternity. If any action did not reflect this, God would punish the perpetrators. Sculptors depicted God as the Supreme Judge.

The Augustinian Order became established in the extreme south of France. St Rufus Abbey, near Avignon, was founded January 1039[13] and adopted the rule about 1070. No houses were founded in Normandy until about 1119.[14]

In 1120 some Augustinian canons sought a stricter rule of life and followed the example of the monastery at Prémontré (Latin - *Præmonstratum*) situated about two miles (about 3km) from Laon, living the more austere way of life of the monks at Cîteaux. Thus evolved the Premonstratensian canons, who like the Cistercian monks, adopted the white habit. The Augustinians became known as the black canons (from the colour of their habit) and the Premonstratensians as the white canons.

At the second Council of the Lateran (1139), pope Innocent II ordained that all regular canons (those living in a strict community) should submit to the rule of St Augustine.

## Early Augustinian Houses in England

Three essentials were necessary for founding a successful monastery:

(1) Sufficient brethren to form a community,

(2) Adequate endowments to ensure self-sufficiency,

(3) A site with potential.

Many of the Augustinian foundations were too small, most consisting of a prior and 11 canons. From these, officials had to be found to manage the community. (See Chapter 9 – Administration Within – Obedientiaries).

Sufficient endowments often came from Norman court circles where it was fashionable to become the patron of one of the new Augustinian foundations. Over three quarters of all houses founded in Henry I's reign were established by officials of his court.[15]

Perhaps the most important factor was a suitable site. The highest spot was not always the best because adequate water supplies were necessary to drive the mill, for washing and to provide drainage. Many monasteries had to move from their original site, some because it was a town site with no room to expand, or too near another monastery and the sound of their bells was confusing, or in a valley with constant rain, or in a drought area.

Few Augustinian houses achieved the status of an abbey and most were administered by a prior, hence a priory. Royal foundations, such as Cirencester and Waltham were abbeys. By 1200 there were 165 Augustinian houses and eight hospitals in England and Wales. The final total was 276.

As well as Merton there were four other Augustinian houses in Surrey, at Newark, Reigate, Southwark and Tandridge, as well as a hospital at Sandon (Esher), whose brethren also followed the Augustinian Rule.

### The First Houses in England

One of the first houses in England to follow the Augustinian Rule was St Botolph, Colchester, in about 1104, with perhaps an earlier contender at Huntingdon. There were clerks living a full common life at St Mary's Huntingdon as early as about 1088 but not following the Augustinian Rule until about 1106,[16] by which time Gilbert the Norman was sheriff of the county (see next chapter).

In Cambridge, sheriff Picot and his wife Hugolina founded a small house of regular canons at the church of St Giles on the south side of the castle. It was colonised from Huntingdon where the subprior Geoffrey was appointed the first prior of Cambridge about 1092.[17] When Gilbert the Norman became sheriff of the county about 1105, he was also castellan of the castle and found only six secular canons at St Giles and the monastery "desolate and reduced to nothing".[18] Together with Pain Peverell, probably the Picots' son-in-law, they planned to increase the community to 30. But these numbers would give rise to other problems for there was insufficient room to provide adequate buildings. In 1112 Gilbert secured a site, from the king, of 13 acres (5.25 ha) "about the spring of Barnwell", and the foundation moved to the new site.[19] Barnwell became the largest religious house in Cambridge.[20]

As sheriff of Cambridgeshire and Huntingdonshire Gilbert had become fully aware of the Augustinian Order and now turned to his other shire, Surrey.

*Merton priory tile designs*
*Dennis Turner (SAC 64 (1967) p.47)*
*(reproduced by permission)*

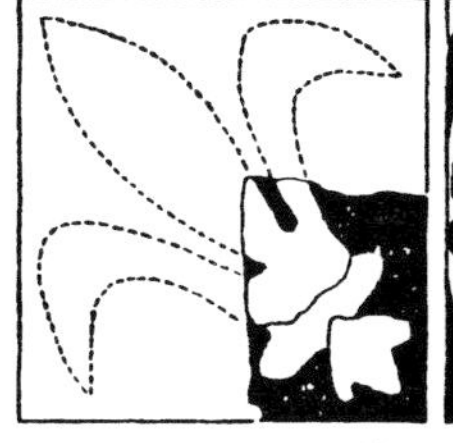

46

48

54-6

*St Mary's church, Merton Park*
*chancel roof – the responsibility of Merton priory*
*Photograph by W A Cook.*

# 1. Gilbert the Founder

*"Good order is the foundation of all good things."*
E Burke *Reflections on the Revolution*

## Merton Priory – The Beginnings

In 1114 Henry I rewarded Gilbert for his services and gave the *ville* of Merton for him "to possess freely in hereditary right".[21] There was already a church in Merton but the Normans despised Saxon buildings and Gilbert built a new church at his own expense, adorning it with pictures and ornaments.

*The parish church that Gilbert built at Merton from a view by Wm. Ellis 1793 (reproduced by courtesy of the Wimbledon Society)*

The *ville* was flourishing, with two mills, land supporting some 21 plough-teams, ten acres of meadow land and woodland sufficient to feed about 800 pigs.[22] Gilbert wished to found a monastery at Merton and sought advice and aid from Huntingdon where the canons "to his knowledge had diffused around the odour of good works".[23] In December 1114 the subprior arrived with a few brethren to settle at Merton, at "the church which had been built".[23] Gilbert endowed the church "with adjacent land sufficient for two ploughs and a mill worth 60*s* [£3] p.a.".[23] Trade with the continent had increased when the Normans arrived and traders favoured London. The nearness of Merton to London, with a good Roman road, must have been a factor in the success of Gilbert's new priory.

The founder then "sought royal licence for the establishment of the monastery, which the king granted as freely as it was asked".[23] The first buildings were of wood and sheriff Gilbert "freehandedly built his priory".[24] This does not mean that he cut the timber and tiled the roof but that he was involved in the layout and design. He built it with the assistance of his household and servants.[23]

Soon, individuals from various parts of England not only bestowed their goods upon the new monastery but entered Merton priory as novices.[25] Matilda (Maud), queen of Henry I, took a great interest and visited Merton.

## Merton Priory – Relocated

After two years, Robert the prior decided that a better site for a monastery would be on the River Wandle a mile away, as there was no river near the new church. He feared suggesting a move to the founder who had spent so much already, so he shared his thoughts with Gilbert's friends. When the founder learnt of Robert's ideas he generously offered to pay for a second foundation. The two men went to the new site "on foot, and on horseback, marking out the space for a church".[26] They measured the bounds for the cemetery and decided how to change the course of the river, and where the mill was to be relocated. The site for the vineyard was chosen, and where the precinct wall should be built.

In setting the bounds of the new priory, Gilbert would have been mindful of the river Wandle, an important feature demarcating parishes. In particular, the communities of Wimbledon, Mitcham and Morden enjoyed the use of meadows, pastures, marshes, fishing and mill ponds. Across the new site was a section of Roman road which provided a firm base for buildings.

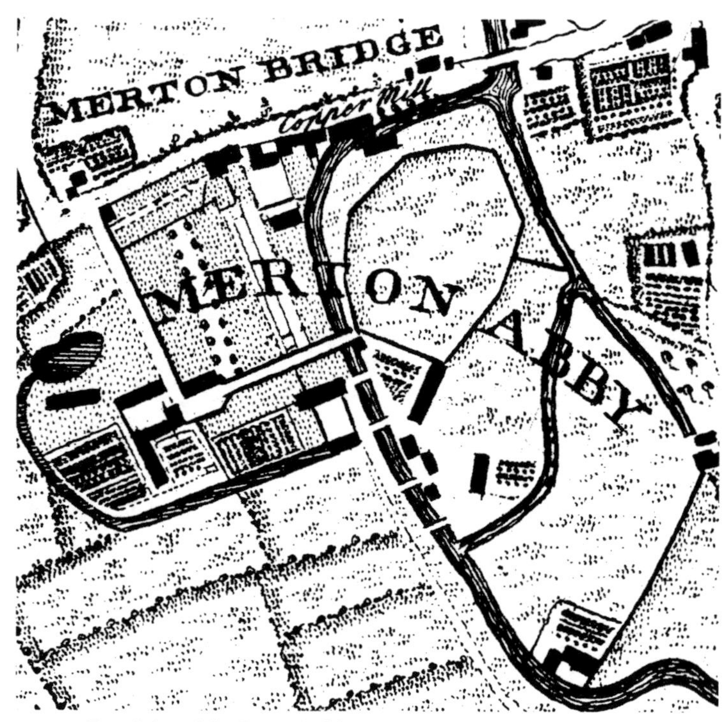

*Detail from John Rocque's Map of 16 miles around London 1745*

Some of the cells and part of the cloister were then transported from the earlier settlement[27] and a wooden church was constructed.[28] Merton was in the diocese of Winchester and the bishop, William Giffard, travelled to bless the new cemetery. On the way he encountered a boy about to be deprived of his sight as punishment for theft, and intervened with his pastoral staff (crosier). The boy was released, which was seen as an omen "that in the place which he came to consecrate, many should be rescued from darkness ... and be brought ... to the light of justice".[24] On Ascension Day in 1117 the canons "entered their new habitation".[24]

The founder worked assiduously to secure for the house the support of the magnates of the realm. He had many influential friends and well-wishers and invited bishops and nobles to see the new foundation. Queen Matilda visited Merton again and, as a dutiful mother, brought prince William.[29] This would have been a difficult time for the first canons, and they had to rely on the charity of the founder, who sent them daily gifts of bread, wine, meat, fish and cheese.[30]

## Merton Priory – Foundation Charter

Gilbert wished to endow his monastery with the royal *ville* or estate of Merton, and sought the king's permission, as well as a foundation charter. He promised Henry a large sum, a hundred pounds in silver and six marks in gold, but the king said it was not enough. The king was holding a Council and Gilbert invited prior Robert to accompany him to Winchester whilst the Merton brethren prayed for the success of their endeavours. The founder had drafted a charter for the priory which contained far-ranging liberties, and the royal legal advisers were afraid to show it to the king.

Gilbert and the prior were also fearful that they had asked for too much and the king would reject the charter. Gilbert then "skilfully courted [the former chancellor] bishop Roger of Salisbury, and asked him to discuss the document's content with the king. The bishop sympathised with the priory's plight".[31] Gilbert's friendship with Roger probably began at the Exchequer where Gilbert had become the senior sheriff in England and was able to hold his ground when dealing with the officials at the Treasury.[32]

When King Henry complained that no jurisdiction was reserved for him and no service to him, the bishop replied that by giving freely to God he would receive more abundant blessings. So Gilbert succeeded in obtaining the *ville* for the monastery, and he called the inhabitants together to inform them that they were now serving the priory.

The charter of 1121[33] reserved royal protection to the monastery when built and as a royal foundation opened the way for royal and other benefactors to grant it churches, manors, mills, land, woods and fisheries. The charter was witnessed by the two archbishops, 15 bishops, and five earls, as well as the king, the queen and Roger of Salisbury. It gave assurance that the fame of the monastery would be extensive.[34] Several bishops came at various times to celebrate the divine mysteries and give benediction.[35]

Gilbert visited the priory often, and sat and talked with the prior or in his absence any canon, if talking was permitted.[35] At length the time arrived when all debts and liabilities had been paid.[36]

## A Monument in Stone

The founder was now caught up in a reforming zeal which emanated from Burgundy and was sweeping the Church. A new style of expansive building, following that of Cluny, began to appear in England at Lewes (1077 or 1081) and Bermondsey (1089). When Cluny enlarged their church 1088-1108, the prior of Lewes decided to follow suit and remodel his, although it was not commenced until about 1140, with an additional eastern transept containing chapels. Gilbert no doubt desired to build similarly at Merton.

In March 1125 the founder began a church "of vast, handsome and powerful workmanship [*amplissimi speciosissimi et fortissimi operis*], the first stone of which he laid himself in the presence of the brethren with holy water, the cross and tapers. The prior placed the second stone, and each brother laid individual stones, and thus what was prayed for came into being".[37] But to some, the work was too ambitious and costly, and work ceased after the founder's death. Even the finished work was nearly all destroyed except the façade and the foundation where Gilbert laid the first stone.[37]

This was probably the last occasion for the founder to be present at Merton, for within four months he had died.

*Foundation arch of infirmary building, looking north (1990)*
*(photograph by the author by permission of the site director)*
*A method introduced about 1290, with arches linking piers of stone and the whole brought to a level surface below ground level. Less stone was required and the amount of digging was reduced. No cellar was intended.*

## 2. Gilbert the Norman

*"Kind hearts are more than coronets,*
*And simple faith than Norman blood."*
Lord Tennyson *Lady Clara Vere de Vere*

Gilbert was born in Normandy soon after 1066 (the Norman Conquest),[38] came from "a generous line of nobility and [was] bred as a soldier".[39] When a boy of his rank reached the age of seven or eight he would have been fostered out to a castellan to be brought up together with the sons of other knights in a castle. He was given menial household tasks to do, and as he grew older would have looked after horses and the livery. It was customary for young men of good birth to be trained to be a knight, as this would be a way to display talent and could eventually lead to rewards in the form of land.

Knights were below the highest rank of aristocracy but learned how to look after themselves, being equipped with horse and armour. It was essential for a knight to be physically fit and strong when the chain-mail alone could weigh about 15 kg (33 lb) – all hung from the shoulders – and he had to wield a heavy sword.

Gilbert may have entered England in 1085 (aged about 18) when a large army of mounted men and infantry was brought over by William to meet a Danish threat.[40]

A new aristocracy arose in England, all speaking Norman-French. As expatriates they had a strong sense of ancestry and family loyalties. The knights came to be known by their first name followed by their patronym which was often their place of residence.[41] Gilbert's father died early in his life.[42] Gilbert's surname is a strange one since Normans were everywhere. The name Normannus meant literally 'northman', so he may have been of Norse descent and not a Dane or a Germanic Frank.

There were many kinds of duties a young knight owed to his lord, some of which were civil rather than military. A knight's civil duties included attending the lord's court, helping to administer justice in his local courts and minor legal matters such as witnessing documents. Thus a knight had authority in local government and became a leader in county society.

When Henry I became king in 1100 his military household consisted of a professional corps of young knights who "formed the shock-troops around whom the bands of mercenaries and those fighting to fulfil their feudal duties gathered".[43]

Gilbert was now witnessing important changes in methods of governing England. Henry began to select men to specialise in either the judiciary or in his new office of the Exchequer. He appointed 'new' men in the shires who could keep a tight financial control, rather than continuing to nominate members of the aristocracy.

Hugh of Buckland was the existing sheriff of London, Middlesex and most of the home counties north of the Thames. Haimo II was sheriff of Kent and Roger of Huntingdon was sheriff of Cambridgeshire, Huntingdonshire and Surrey. Soon after 1104 Gilbert was made sheriff of Huntingdonshire,[44] and of the other two shires.[45]

Gilbert's biographer remarks that "as though to extend the glory of God, he had been promoted to the honour of sheriff of the county".[46] Each year the sheriffs paid the royal dues of their counties into the Lower Exchequer at Westminster and received wooden tallies marked with notches as receipts. At the Upper Exchequer they were questioned about their accounts. A sheriff was often brutal, exacting the most from the peasant, or else lenient and inefficient. Gilbert's fearless attitude to the examiners at the Exchequer suggests that for 20 years he found a middle way. The king, who used to treat his sheriffs with insults and abuse, respected Gilbert and never directed harsh words toward him.[47] When Hugh of Buckland died about 1116, Gilbert was probably the longest serving sheriff, and "perhaps the best-loved magnate of the day".[48]

Around 1120 Gilbert heard and settled a dispute between the abbots of Thorney and Peterborough.[49] However, later, he made a wrong decision when he took control of the estate of Ranulf the chancellor on his death in January 1123. Ranulf had been a tenant of Westminster Abbey at Battersea and abbot Herbert of the abbey complained. The king issued a writ to the sheriff restoring the estate "particularly that part of the land of which Gilbert unjustly delivered *seisin* (virtually the freehold) to a Hugh FitzHedric".[50]

The splendour and magnificence in which Gilbert lived as a sheriff is highly spoken of, and his hospitality is said to have been so great that his doors were constantly kept open, so that everyone who wished might find ready access and be entertained according to his rank.[39] Whenever possible, there would be 13 paupers dining in his presence.[47]

His piety was inherited from his widowed mother. "She was chaste, pious and sober, such as God loves ... the shameful and lascivious only she did not benefit but rebuked".[36] Gilbert brought his mother to England and at least one of his siblings was perhaps also in England for, on Gilbert's death, Henry I appointed Fulk, a nephew of Gilbert, to be sheriff of the three counties until 1129. Gilbert's mother died probably in 1117, and was buried at Merton.[47] On her death Henry's queen Matilda (Maud) adopted Gilbert in feudal fashion,[51] until she died in 1118, barely 38 years old.

At Huntingdon, Gilbert would often visit the mother house of St Mary's Augustinian priory and also St Neots' priory south of Huntingdon. This was an alien priory belonging to Bec, Normandy, where Gilbert could converse in Norman-French as well as Latin with the prior and brethren, and refresh ancestral loyalties.

In 1124 there was a famine in England and Gilbert's men, overseers of the king's lands, reported to him that the poor were stealing the king's crops and trampling them.

Even when beaten and chased away, they returned because of their hunger. Gilbert showed his humanity by ordering his men to stop harassing the poor and allow them to eat freely. He gave assurances to the overseers that he would accept full responsibility for the king's lands.[52]

In July 1125 Gilbert realised that he was ill and sent a letter requesting Robert, prior of Merton, to come to him quickly. But his own men prevented the messenger from leaving, fearing that if the prior came Gilbert would leave them to enter the monastery.[53]

Gilbert the Norman died on Sunday 26 July 1125 and John de Escures, bishop of Rochester, agreed to perform the requiem mass. On the night before he came to Merton for this purpose he had a vision of the body before the altar, of a church thronged by paupers.[53] The priors of Huntingdon and St Neots accompanied the body to Merton, and attending the funeral as canons were Stephen, archdeacon of Surrey, and Serlo, former dean of Salisbury.[54]

Gilbert's fiscal accounts were left in perfect order and no debts remained to be paid. The huge sum promised to the king in return for the foundation charter of the priory (see previous chapter), was never fully paid, for Gilbert had flattered the treasury collectors into easing his debt.[55] Only two of Gilbert's household had known that for two or more years prior to his death he bore, as his cross, a thick iron chain over his bare loins.[56]

*Marble head of a royal or noble personage, discovered in 1797 when a portion of the precinct wall collapsed. Sir William Hamilton presented it to the Society of Antiquaries when he lived nearby in 1802. (Photograph reproduced from A Heales –* The Records of Merton Priory *(1898), by courtesy of the Society of Antiquaries.)*

*Plan of the 12th-century priory church at Merton, based partly on archaeological evidence.*
*This shows a lay-out on a grid of 40 Norman feet*

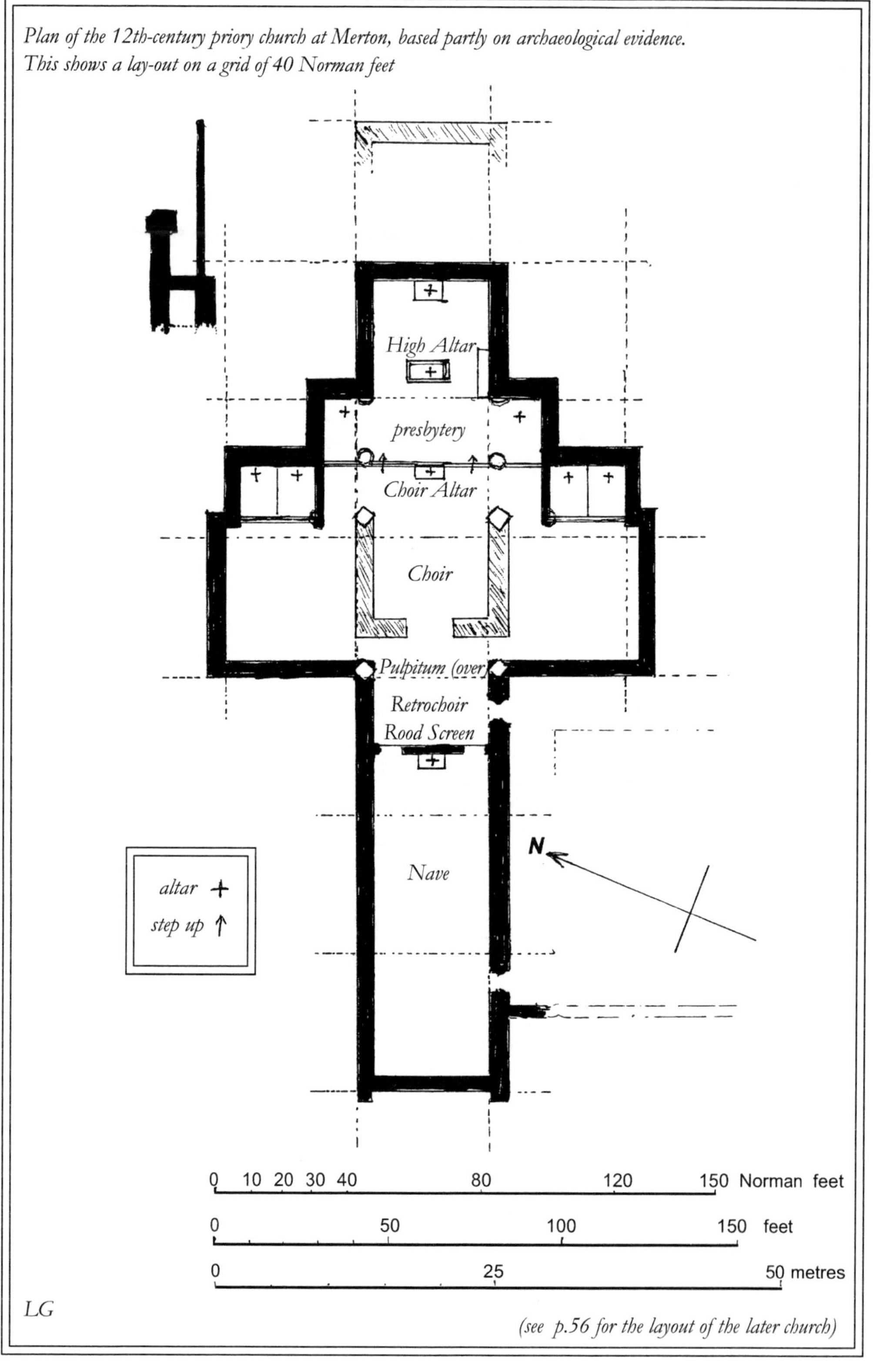


LG

*(see p.56 for the layout of the later church)*

## 3. Early Buildings

*"Always present your front to the world."*
Moliere *L'Avare* Act 3 Scene 1

The magnificent building planned by Gilbert was halted on his death and the first completed stone church was a simple structure which probably followed the design of a previous timber church, with a square ended chancel and gabled roof. This building was completed in the 1130s, for the record says: " Finally after fifteen years, the monastic structures were peacefully constructed with the aid of the faithful at different times according to their will and means".[57]

The late John Harvey offered the opinion that early Norman buildings in England seem to have been set out with either Norman or Roman feet.[58] One Norman foot was 11 11/16 inches or 297.77mm. It was fairly simple for the master mason to lay out lines on the ground and all measurements were from one wall face to another on the same side and not centre to centre, although the measurement is likely to be the same. An early layout at Merton appears to follow a grid pattern made up of squares of 40 Norman feet or roughly twelve metres. This church contained north and south transepts with chapels in the eastern aisles, a presbytery with short aisles on both sides, and a nave without aisles.

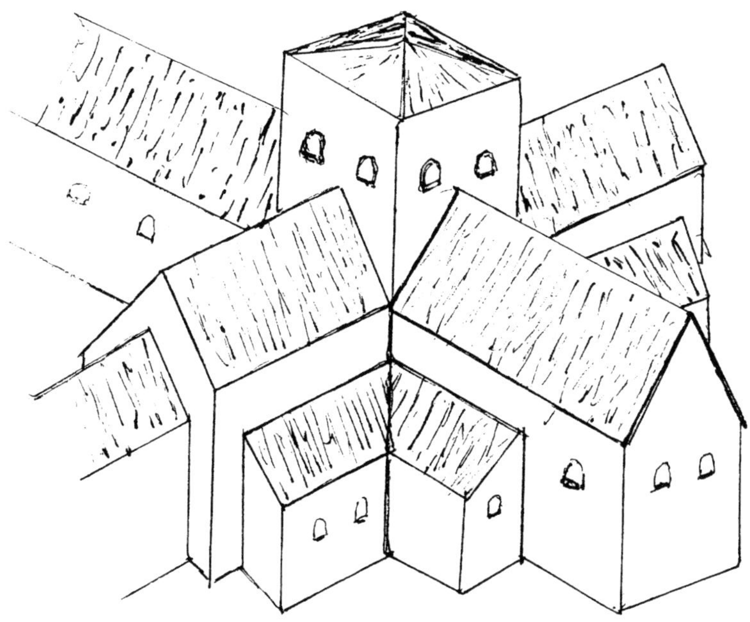

*Conjectural perspective view of the early priory church from the south-east* *LG*

According to one of his biographers, it was the influence of Thomas Becket that encouraged one building phase. As chancellor to, and friend of, Henry II in 1154, Becket persuaded the king to pay for further building work. "The lord king again received into grace and friendship the canonical church of Merton…and at his own cost completed the existing building from the choir and transepts, which had already been constructed, and enriched it with perpetual revenues".[59]

On 23rd May 1162, in the refectory at Westminster abbey, Thomas Becket was elected archbishop of Canterbury without opposition. He immediately rode to Merton, not only to see the new work but also to adopt the habit of a canon. Becket then asked canon Robert, probably a contemporary at the priory school, to be his confessor.[60]

In 1162/3 Henry II gave £26 13s 4d (£26.66) "for the works of the church",[61] and in 1165 the priory borrowed a similar amount from William Cade, a moneylender. The loan was made upon the security of Merton's vineyard at Sutton.[62] Also in 1165 the king granted many further liberties to the priory.[63]

The only record of progress can be found from the dates that the various altars were dedicated. In 1161 that of the infirmary chapel,[61] the altar of St John the Baptist in 1174,[64] the altars of St Stephen and St Nicholas "in the priory church" in 1194 and that of the Holy Cross in 1197.[65] The rebuilding was completed in time for many national occasions beginning with king John's visit in June 1204 with the archbishop, bishops and earls together with their retinues.[66]

A later rebuilding of the church involved the enlarging and moving the transepts to the east. This increased the length of the nave. A larger and higher building was envisaged, and the only known way to obtain height was by increasing the breadth of the nave. Thus aisles were added and arcades of eight bays constructed. The addition of the south aisle affected the size of the cloister, as did the displacement of the south transept.

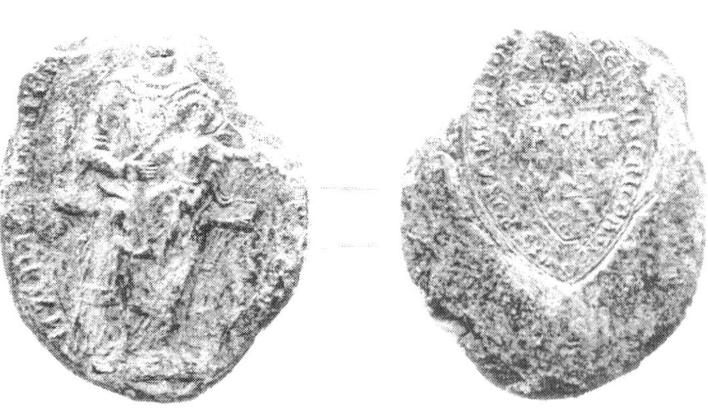

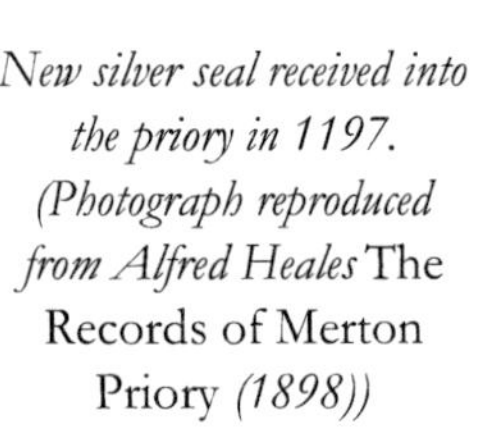

*New silver seal received into the priory in 1197. (Photograph reproduced from Alfred Heales* The Records of Merton Priory *(1898))*

## 4. Augustinian Canons

*"A cord of three strands is not quickly broken."*
Ecclesiastes 4:12

Those committed to a life in a monastery entered as oblates or postulants and were placed on probation before taking any vows. Once accepted, they entered the noviciate and studied for the minor orders under the master of the novices for at least a year.[67] The novice master was often the precentor of the priory. At the completion of this training they made their vows of poverty, chastity and obedience, and they received the minor order of acolyte. They could now claim to be in minor orders although not yet canons. They underwent further instruction and examination and received the first tonsure. The shape of the bald patch was the 'trade mark' of the order. Subsequent ordination was on the prior's recommendation which took them to sub-deacons and then deacons (probationary priests). Only the bishop could ordain them as a canon and priest. Some canons obtained a master's degree and took the title *magister*. Long-serving canons were known as the elders or s*eniores et saniores* (senior and wiser). They would know the precise boundaries of the priory's lands and could say how the community had overcome major problems such as famines and plagues.

Augustinian canons, being priests, were able to serve at churches where the priory held the advowson (the right to appoint the incumbent). Merton held so many that this was impracticable and vicars were appointed as parish priests. The ordered life in the cloisters was always preferred to performing parochial work.[68]

Although the basic framework within which the canons passed their lives remained largely unchanged over hundreds of years, details of their existence were frequently rethought. Over the years monasticism adapted itself to contemporary economic, social and political development.

### Recruitment

At Merton some oblates came from afar, attracted by the prestige of the new found monastery, but many came from the manors and estates now owned by the priory.[69]

Only tenants without feudal obligations could be considered as oblates, which ruled out many of the local inhabitants. Recruits often came from the nobility, who used the existence of monasteries to solve their inheritance problems. They were always concerned about maintaining their position in society and the obligation that all oblates had to lead a celibate life was a means of restricting procreation, which reduced the risk of impoverishment of the family. The feudal rule of primogeniture prevented the division of inheritance, but did not resolve the problem of occupations for younger brothers. There was certainly class distinction within the Augustinian order – more than in the other orders.[70] At the General Chapter of the order in

1276, it was agreed that "special seats are to be allocated to those who have been rich ... or are of noble birth".[71] Being of the educated class, all canons would be expected to have servants.

The size of establishment in Augustinian houses in the early medieval period was usually between 26 and 36.[72]

**Number of brethren at Merton priory**

| Date | Prior | Other Canons | Subdeacons & Deacons | Acolytes | Scholars | Total | Source |
|---|---|---|---|---|---|---|---|
| 1114 | 1 | | | | | a few | |
| 1117 | 1 | 15 | | | | 16 | Colker (70) 242 |
| 1121 | 1 | 23 | | | | 24 | Colker (70) 243 |
| 1125 | 1 | 35 | | | | 36 | Colker (70) 245 |
| 1314 | | "numbers had fallen" (*Registrum Henrici Woodlock* I .75) | | | | | |
| | | Establishment | | | | 40 | Heales 269 |
| 1387 | 1 | 28 | | | | 29 | Heales 269 |
| | | "40 canons were accustomed to dwell devoutly ... now hardly exist thirty" | | | | | |
| 1485 | 1 | 17 | - | - | 2 | 20 | Heales 303/4 |
| 1492 | 1 | 22 | - | 2 | - | 25 | Heales 309 |
| 1501 | 1 | 19 | - | - | - | 20 | K & H 146* |
| 1502 | 1 | 13 | 5 | 3 | - | 22 | Heales 311 |
| 1510 | Bishop enjoined prior "to fill up fully and perfectly the ancient number of canons *viz.* to 28 inclusive" | | | | | | Heales 320 |
| 1520 | 1 | 14 | 1 | 1 | 4 | 21 | Heales 324 |
| 1530 | 1 | 12 | 3 | 1 | 4 | 21 | Heales 330/1 |
| 1535 | 1 | 17 | - | - | 2 (dismissed) | 20 | Heales 340 |
| 1538 | 1 | 13 | - | - | 1 | 15 | Heales 349 |

*K & H = D Knowles & R Hadcock *Medieval Religious Houses* ... 1953

*Merton priory tile designs (reproduced by courtesy of MoLAS and the London Borough of Merton)*

## Dress

Each canon wore a long black cassock which was lined with sheepskin during the winter months. Over this he wore a knee-length white linen rochet (resembling a surplice) with wide sleeves gathered at the wrists. Over the shoulders was the amice or short cape which in later years was joined at the breast and had to be put over the head. The amice was worn in the cloister with a black skull cap covering the tonsured head. Underclothes consisted of a doublet, breeches and white stockings.

All slept in their clothes, and the bishop of Winchester, following a visitation on 27 September 1387, admonished the brethren when he suspected that "some canons sleep without drawers or shirts, contrary to the rules of observance … The prior or sub-prior, under pain of suspension [were] to enquire sharply and not postpone punishment of offenders".[73] A protest was sent to the bishop denying that such a manner of sleeping was indulged in.

In the cloister they wore woollen shoes or slippers and sometimes latchet sandals. Outside the monastery they often wore gaiters (*ocre*) and top boots (*bote*) i.e. not tight hose (*calige*).[74] The *capa nigra* or black cope was the 'habit' worn outside the house and gave them the popular title of Black Canons. Headgear evolved and became a square cap, although Doctors of Divinity wore their special cap.

*An Augustinian canon in the 16th century from W Dugdale's* Monasticon Anglicanum

## Diet

Egg-foods formed an important part of the diet. In 1492 at St Swithun's Winchester, 3,944 eggs were consumed in 36 days in a community similar to Merton (35 brothers). However this is only three eggs per monk per day excluding guest requirements.[75]

Fish was a large item on the menu and in addition to freshwater fish bred in the stew ponds, marine fish brought from the east coast ports were always available. These included plaice, cod and herring and the last two could be preserved by smoking or salting and dried for winter use. By 1300, hake and haddock were introduced as cod and herring became scarce.

Additional choices of food following the pottage (a kind of thick soup or stew) were often provided, especially at festivals. These were known as pittances. For these items the kitchener would unlock the spice chest. Spices were an important ingredient in meals.

As well as the meals provided, each canon was allowed daily the 'great convent miche' (loaf) and 1½ gallons (nearly 7 litres) of beer.[76]

### Travel

Augustinian canons were often asked to travel on royal business. In 1205 king John wrote to the bailiffs of Portsmouth commanding them to assist the passage of Ralph de Plesseto and a canon of Merton, "ambassadors of the king, whom he sends to Normandy upon his affairs". They were to take no one with them "but their domestics and that they take neither arms nor saddle-horses".[77]

This confirms that from an early period the canons had servants, who travelled with them on journeys.

### Death of a canon

To the dying the prior administered the last rites and all the brethren were summoned to the infirmary by a canon striking a hanging board with a mallet. In the infirmary there was often a special stone which was covered with sackcloth and ashes[78] in the form of a cross. On this was placed the dying canon with the brethren kneeling around him.

After death, the body was washed and removed to the infirmary chapel whilst all recited the Litany of the Dying. It was incensed before being removed to the priory church for a requiem mass.

Here a framework of wood or metal was placed over the dead body, fitted with prickets for requiem candles. They recall the teeth of the harrow and the structure was known as a *herse* (French for harrow). The canons grouped themselves round the herse and set candles or torches. A knell was rung.

The burial ceremony began with the antiphon *placebo* (Psalm 116:9 *Placebo Domino in regione vivorum*) and continued with the *dirige*[79] (Psalm 5:8. *Dirige Domine me, in conspectu tuo vitam meum*).

The funeral procession made its way to the canons' cemetery where the canons stood around the open grave as the body, sewn in linen cloth or placed in a wooden coffin, was lowered into the earth.

*The elaborate* herse *for the funeral of abbot Islip at Westminster Abbey 1532. (Reproduced* from Vetusta Monumenta, *Society of Antiquaries IV (1815) by courtesy of the Society of Antiquaries)*

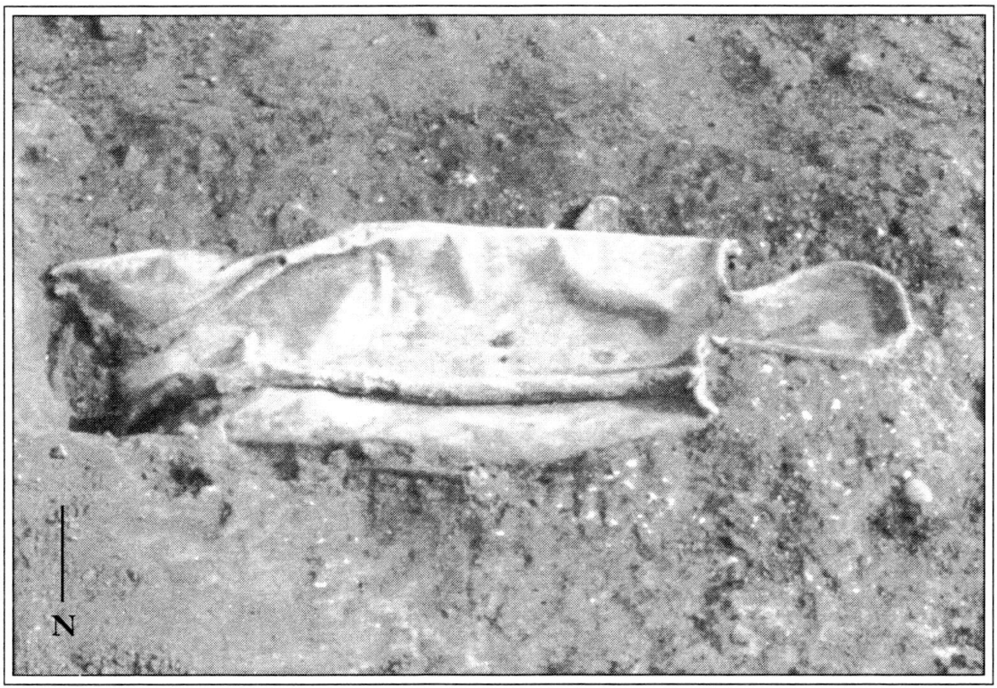


*A lead coffin found during excavations at the Priory church in 1987 (Photograph by W J Rudd by permission of the site director)*

## Archæology of the Cemetery

Over 700 skeletons of burials at Merton priory were excavated between 1976 and 1990. Some interesting conclusions have been made from a study of these bones where there was "a larger proportion of the elderly than at other monastic sites" (around London).[80] This demonstrates the longevity of Merton canons, but in turn reveals that many skeletons showed signs of deformity where extra bone formed on the spine and often the vertebrae had fused together. About 10% of samples excavated from monastic sites in London show signs of this disease known as DISH.[81]

**D** Disseminated – spread widely.

**I** Idiopathic – not occasioned by another disease.

**S** Skeletal – relating to the framework of the body.

**H** Hyperostosis – overgrowth of bony tissue.

Approximately half the skeletons from the chapter house area had *hyperostosis* of the femur, knee, ankle and heel. The deformity may have been caused through consuming too much animal fat (containing vitamin A). Another contributory factor of late-onset diabetes has been suggested.

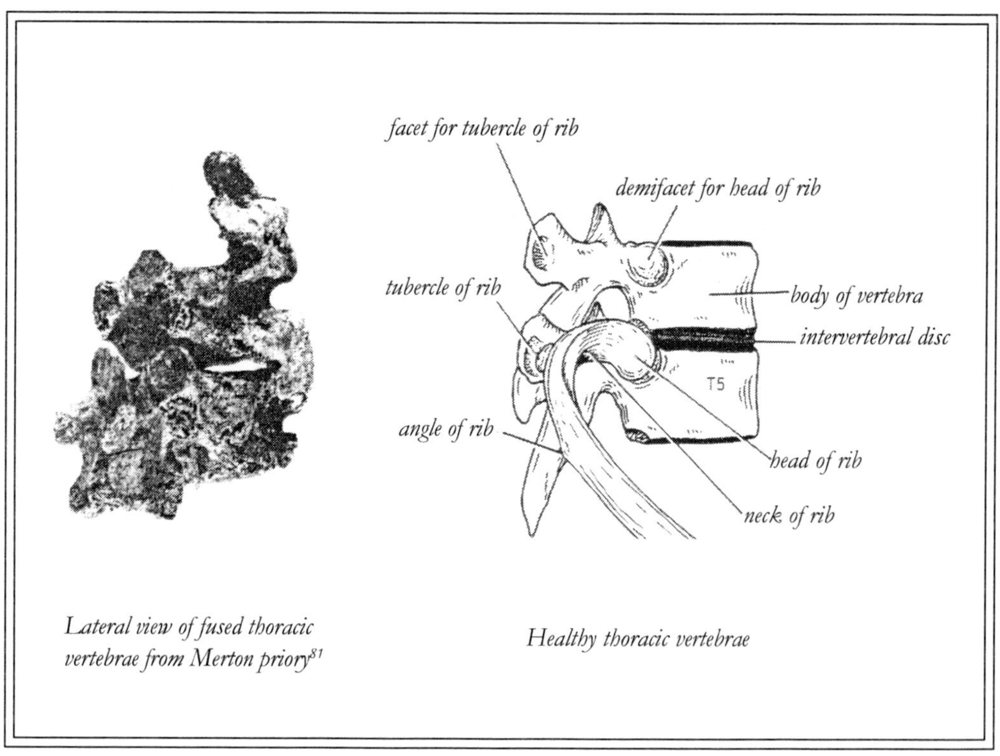


*Lateral view of fused thoracic vertebrae from Merton priory*[81]

*Healthy thoracic vertebrae*

# 5. The Prior

*"… the greatest among you should be like the youngest,*
*and the one who rules like the one who serves."*
Luke 22:26

At the head of the establishment was the prior. He was responsible for the direction of the house, and to him all the brethren owed obedience. Inside and outside the precinct the prior was all important.

To hold the office of a prior it was necessary to be a free man (as were all monks and canons), a priest of lawful age, born of lawful wedlock, to have a knowledge of 'letters and manners' and to be wise in 'spiritual and temporal' matters. The superior of a monastery was in touch with men of all ranks of society – from country gentlemen, yeomen, artisans, craftsmen, peasants to the poor at the gate. As landowners they were concerned with crops and the weather. They were involved with the care of property and not devoid of a sense of beauty and grandeur in their churches and other buildings.

They were often asked to head commissions of peace and had to rule impartially on disputes between religious houses. The king sometimes requested them to act as messengers, which could involve a journey of some months, even to Rome. Prior Gilbert de Aette was granted a licence for letters of protection for travelling abroad, which was valid from March until 29 August 1273.[82]

## Journeys Often

The grant of so many estates to the priory laid great responsibilities on the prior. He was lord of various manors and, although he appointed stewards and bailiffs to act for him, he was ultimately responsible for dispensing justice, collecting tithes, repairing roads and bridges etc. For royal courts the prior was allowed to appoint attorneys for either prosecution or defence. They were often canons from the priory and acted in county assizes and eyres, and at hundred courts. The prior had his own stables at Merton.[83]

The prior was frequently in London on business and Merton was one of the first monasteries to build a town-house (*hospitium*), if not in the City, at least just over the river at Southwark. Inns did not exist in London before the reign of Edward I (1274-1307)[84] and Merton was granted a large plot of land near the church of St Olave, Southwark, called *Grimscroft*. This was secured in the 1130s from the monks of Rochester,[85] perhaps through the beneficence of bishop John de Escures (d.1137) a friend of Gilbert the founder of Merton.[86] Between 1150 and 1155 it was leased to Simon Dane, a former servant, on condition that the canons could use their *hospitium* when necessary. The rental from Simon was a pound of cinnamon per year. About 1220 the "lord of that fee whom the priory had to satisfy" was Lobulus[87] with the priory paying ground rent (*landgabulum*) of 7½d (3p) per annum. The site was then granted to Arnold the Vintner, but Merton retained the right for their reception when they wished.[87]

The idea of monasteries having a town-house became popular and Merton disposed of their property to Battle abbey about 1225.[88] Sometime between 1239 and 1247, Battle abbey granted land to Eswy who was to pay Merton an annual rent of 6s 8d (33p).

## Election of a New Prior

At the death of the superior there was a strict procedure to be adopted, and certain occasions were identified by Alfred Heales.[89]

All the priory's property was immediately vested in the king until he released it to the new prior. A day was set aside for an election which took place with the bishop's legal representative present. It began with a mass of the Holy Ghost at the high altar of the priory church. A bell was rung to summon all to the chapter house where the assembled knelt and sang the hymn *Come Holy Ghost* … followed by a specified versicle and collect. The director (usually the sub-prior), notaries and witnesses were nominated, proxies announced and confirmed. These were for those sick and others not able to be present. Those not entitled to vote were asked to leave. The director read the royal licence for the election to proceed and the method for election as laid down in the priory's constitution. The canons had complete freedom of choice. All knelt once more and "besought God, by the grace of the Holy Spirit to illumine and inspire their hearts …". If the choice seemed obvious, the matter could be decided by acclamation without voting.

Following the election, the director announced the results. All processed to the church reciting psalm 67 *God be merciful unto us, and bless us* with the prior-elect at the rear of the procession. At the high altar the *Te Deum* was chanted (*We praise thee O God*) and the sub-prior said a prayer for the person being elected. The director then published the result of the election "in a loud and distinct voice". It was a big day for the people of Merton. We can imagine the villagers at the doors between the nave and the choir trying to peer through the crevices to catch glimpses of the proceedings, knowing what was being done, but unable to understand the Latin pronouncements.

At about noon the community returned to the chapter house and proctors were nominated to inform the bishop of the election and perform "all necessary acts for its confirmation". Meanwhile the prior-elect would demur and ask the proctors to elect a more worthy candidate. At length he would seek time for deliberation.

Canonical 'hours' continued until after *nones* when the proctors searched out the chosen one "and there again, urgently, more urgently, and most urgently asked for his consent". He replied "that he was unwilling further to resist the divine will", and a deputation including the prior-elect travelled to the king to obtain his assent. The king and the monastery applied to the bishop for confirmation of the appointment. The bishop replied to the king, asking him to restore temporalities (property) to the prior-elect and chapter. The king ordered the release by his escheator and as his feudal lord received homage from the prior-elect.

Installation by the bishop was another important occasion. The prior-elect was examined by the bishop to ensure that he was competently literate and suitably submissive. All assembled in the priory church and at the west door of the church the bishop received the prior-elect who removed his sandals and walked barefoot in procession to meet all the brethren. At the high altar, the decree of election and the letters of the king giving licence to elect, and assent when made, were all read out. The bishop inducted the elect and confirmed that he now had "the care and administration of the said monastery", handed to him the keys and ordered the obedience of the canons. The archdeacon made the public announcement. All joined in the *Te Deum* and the bells rang out a peal.

The prior knelt at the high altar with the bishop praying over him and giving the episcopal benediction. The bishop raised the prior giving him the kiss of peace and blessing him. The prior now made his profession of canonical obedience to the bishop.[89]

### Called to account

The 15th prior Edmund de Herierd (1296-1305) was excommunicated in 1300 for paying money for the King's use despite the Pope's interdict.[90] He was released from exclusion on 4 May 1301 but proved to be a weak leader. On 25 September 1305 he offered his resignation as prior, on the grounds of disagreements, which was accepted by the bishop.

At the forthcoming election in December Herierd was again nominated, together with William de Brokesborn. The bishop was not able to intervene because one of the proctors maintained his right to proceed with the election regardless. Both the king (Edward I) and the convent, led by the sub-prior, wrote to the bishop and asked him to appoint a prior. Even the archbishop joined in and decided that Herierd had caused serious trouble and ordered him to resume life as a canon of Merton. On 5 March 1306 the bishop chose a new man, which probably pleased no one.

### Finance

Although the prior kept his financial affairs separate from the monastery, it was the custom for his accounts to be presented to the brethren at chapter twice a year. In 1509 at the bishop's visitation, it was found that prior William Salinge had not done this and he was asked "to deliver up and leave in the chapter house, his book of accounts for the space of a month for full consideration".[91]

*An Augustinian teacher*
*Based on Oxford, Bodleian Library, MS. Laud Misc. 409, fo.3v – late 12th century – depicting Hugh of St Victor, d.1142, one of the first masters to teach theology to students in Paris.*

## 6. Centre of Learning

*"Let the little children come to me … for the kingdom of God belongs to such as these."*
Luke 18:16

### School for Novices

Every monastery had a novice-master to ensure that candidates for professing to the Order received suitable training. This was of utmost importance for the future well-being of the monastery and the task was entrusted to a senior canon. There were never more than six novices at a time and the novice-master had to show sympathy as well as control.

Novices were taught singing and chanting for services in the choir, the observance of the Rule and customs in church, dormitory, refectory and cloister.

They learnt the psalter by heart in Latin and, as they progressed, learnt grammar, philosophy, theology and music.

### Song-school

Children under the age of ten were considered to possess a potential for closeness to God and every monastery ran a song-school. The children were seen to have attributes of trust, sincerity, openness and dependency. Most large monasteries supported both a song-school and an almonry school. The latter found its most convenient site adjacent to the great gateway,[92] and kept apart from the canons. The almoner gave elementary education without commitment that a child should become a postulant.

### Children of the Cloister

Early monasteries accepted the practice for the nobility to send sons there for early education, but these "children of the cloister" disappeared as a class in the 12th century in England.[93] Thereafter, children aged five to seven were only offered to monasteries by parents as oblates and future members of the community.

Merton was fortunate in that one of its first canons was an Italian schoolmaster named Guy who must have influenced Merton's becoming a centre for learning. It has been suggested that Nicholas Breakspear was at Merton at the time of Guy,[94] following a suggestion of the abbot of St Albans.[95] Nicholas Breakspear became an Augustinian canon at St Rufus near Avignon, and in 1154 the only Englishman to become pope (Adrian IV).

About 1130 Gilbert Becket, portreeve[96] of London, sent his son Thomas to school at Merton, chosen in preference to the three major schools in London mentioned in

FitzStephen's account of the city. Gilbert could have chosen Aldgate priory which was founded before Merton in 1108. In fact some of the canons at Merton may have come from Aldgate.[97]

When Thomas arrived at Merton, the priory church was still a wooden building, as the ambitious stone structure was abandoned after the founder's death in 1125. Some building work continued as the record states that it took 15 years (until 1132) to complete.[98] Thomas would be responsible for the subsequent enlargement of the church after 1154.

David Knowles thought that Thomas had a domineering father who, as a prosperous citizen of London, was used to entertaining court officials.[99] The following anecdote suggests another side to him.

Gilbert came to visit his son at Merton and the boy was brought into the prior's presence. Gilbert fell prone before his son so that prior Robert exclaimed "You foolish old man, what are you doing? The honour you do to him, he ought rather to do to you". Gilbert replied in an undertone, "My lord, I know what I am doing; this boy will be great in the sight of the Lord".[100]

## Education in General

A spirit of learning followed closely in the wake of the revival of monasticism and the Augustinians became prominent educators. The historian Frank Barlow was of the opinion that it was the Augustinian canons who began to take over existing schools as at Huntingdon or established new ones as at Merton.[101] Merton's school was probably similar to the Huntingdon school which the prior had known for eight years. About 1120 Huntingdon priory was given permission to operate a school "so that no one shall keep a school in Huntingdonshire without their leave".[102] The foundation charter of St Gregory, Canterbury (*c.*1145) ensured that a song-school and a grammar school were set up.[103] The purpose of these schools was to provide sufficient education for the student to qualify for ordination or at least to enable him to take matriculation for University.

Edmund Rich, a teacher of distinction, lived in the priory 1213/4 and would have had an influence on Merton's school.

At the beginning of the 13th century Walter de Merton was educated at Merton, where he became a legal clerk assisting the prior in conveyancing property. In return, the prior assisted Walter in setting up a House of the Scholars of Merton at Malden, Surrey, the priory acting as trustee. This was primarily to teach Walter's 13 nephews, but the school was moved to Oxford and Walter secured a charter of incorporation in 1264 with power to maintain 20 scholars at Oxford. This was the first college with its own constitution.

For the Augustinian Order many students went to Osney abbey, Oxford, to study, and it could be said that its school was the first to be connected with the University. Monasteries were the repositories of knowledge until the colleges at universities were founded.

All was not well at Merton in 1387 when the bishop visited and requested the prior to provide a "suitable master to instruct in singing and in other branches of knowledge".[104]

It was decreed that Augustinian houses should enable canons to study at Oxford in the proportion of one for every 20 established canons. A fine of £10 a year was levied by the Provincial Chapter, on monasteries not acting on this. Unfortunately many found it easier to pay the fine than pay for the maintenance of an absent canon, especially as some studied for up to ten years or so.[105] Merton also provided bursaries and lent books to candidates. In 1228 the priory supported John de Tinenwe for 16 years to study, and he could stay at the priory when on vacation or go abroad.[106]

## Guy of Merton

*"A student is not above his teacher, but everyone who is fully trained will be like his teacher."*
Luke 6:40

Guy came from Italy, following in the footsteps of Lanfranc (d.1089) and Anselm (d.1109), who had made the long journey across the Alps before him. In their time they all achieved a remarkable reputation for the direction of schools.[107] However Guy, as far as we know, never taught at Bec Abbey as they had done and did not, like them, become archbishop of Canterbury, but joined Merton priory at its foundation.

There is evidence to believe that Guy was Guido Langobardus, a known philosopher of repute and linked with Lanfranc and others.[108] Guy had a son who was aware of his father's reputation and wrote to Merton priory years later for information. The reply from canon Rainald is preserved in a book which belonged to Merton priory and is now in the British Library (Royal MS 8 E ix fol. 91-98). It must date from between 1133 and 1150 and provides an insight into the life of a canon. Rainald admits that he wrote his letter "between the canonical hours, and often, when I should have been intent on these religious services, I was thinking instead about the composition".[109]

Although Guy was a schoolmaster, he was only in minor orders when he arrived at Merton. The *epistola* (letter) shows how seriously Guy took his noviciate at Merton and how diligently he studied the Customs and Observances. When he decided to become a canon he observed the finer points of them "as if they came from God himself".[110] When prior Robert promoted him to become a deacon Guy protested his "unworthiness" and it was only under compulsion that he accepted the priesthood.

Guy would reprimand himself should his mind wander when reading and meditating. He would sometimes gnash his teeth or dig his nails into his flesh or beat his chest to make his mind more attentive. He humbly told a friend that only twice did he celebrate mass without tears.[110]The letter records that the prior's illness was alleviated through Guy's sanctity and prayers.[111]

He taught and encouraged the brethren at Merton but left to become the first prior of Merton's daughter houses at Taunton (1120) and Bodmin (1123) – (see chapter 7 – Daughter Houses). Guy was back at Merton 1121 to 1123 to the place he loved and was able to continue teaching, free from the constraints of office. He rejoiced "as if freed from a prison or like a bird released from a trap".[112]

The historian Frank Barlow has commented that the career of Guy suggests that the bishops (of Winchester and Exeter) and archbishop (Corbeil) were interested in the furtherance of education as much as the religious life.[113]

Guy set an example for others to follow. Not only those who lived alongside him but for later generations who read about him through this *epistola.*

He returned to Bodmin early in 1124, and was called to discuss a case with bishop Warelwast of Exeter. On the journey to the bishop, Guy's horse bolted throwing him into a pit. His injuries were serious and he was carried to Exeter. To his bedside came his friends from Bodmin and Plympton priories, Algar and Geoffrey, to look after him, but his health deteriorated daily. Guy asked his friends what day it was and when told that it was the vigil of Ascension he declared "Today is the day of my redemption, today is the day of God's compassion … It is the day of my joy".[114] He no doubt recalled Ascension Day 1117 when he first entered Merton priory joyfully.

On Guy's death Algar wished him to be buried at Bodmin, but the canons of Exeter successfully claimed the right to bury Guy and such a multitude flocked together to show veneration as had never been seen in the city, not even for a bishop, within the memory of those present. Guy's body was laid in a stone sarcophagus and set in a place of honour.[115]

We may ask how it was that Rainald, a canon of Merton, came to know the details of Guy's death and funeral. The informant may have been one of Guy's friends and as Rainald's letter states that "Geoffrey looked after the body, since Algar, in tears, could not control his distress",[115] it points to Geoffrey rather than Algar. A canon of Merton could, however, have travelled to Exeter for the funeral.

Geoffrey became the second prior of Plympton in 1128 and may have visited Merton. Algar was made bishop of Coutances in 1132. He also could have visited Merton when he returned from Normandy for the rededication of Exeter cathedral after its rebuilding in 1133.

# 7. Daughter Houses

*"Like mother, like daughter"*
Ezekiel 16:44

The canons of Merton began their ordered lives within the newly built priory on 3 May 1117, and the bishop of Winchester was impressed with the 15 canons and how they were "sublimely aspiring to perfection" after not even three years. Amongst the first brethren of Merton were Stephen, former archdeacon of Surrey, and Serlo former dean of Salisbury[116] (see later under Cirencester). The bishop requested some canons to "introduce into his church of Taunton those same observances which they themselves employed".[117]

This was the beginning of a fine record by Merton priory of setting up daughter houses, but the regular departure of canons from their home foundation must have caused a strain on those remaining and says much about the flow of new recruits. It is difficult to understand where they came from. In 1117 there were 15,[118] but in 1120 five left to found Taunton and early in the following year two or three assisted the canons of Aldgate, London, to found Plympton. But such was the attraction of the mother house that by 1121, new recruits swelled the numbers to 23.[119] Towards the end of 1123 archbishop Corbeil requested Merton canons to go to Canterbury in order that the hospital of St Gregory could follow the Augustinian Order. At the same time, the bishop of Exeter asked for a few canons to introduce the Order to Bodmin. They left Merton under the leadership of *magister* Guy who died on Ascension Day 1124.[120] Recruitment continued and by 1125, numbers were up to 36 or 37.[121] Three years later some canons left Merton for Edinburgh, led by Alwin who became the first abbot of Holyrood. Within 33 years of its foundation, Merton had set up nine Augustinian houses, sending forth bands of missionary brothers to other parts of England and even to Normandy and Scotland.[122]

*Map showing location of daughter houses*

The early daughter houses of Augustinian monasteries were unlike those of the Benedictines in that they were not dependent, but maintained themselves from the outset. The initiative to found a new community came, not from the mother house, but from a local lord or a bishop who requested a few canons from an established and revered community to settle in and lead a new foundation of his own patronage.

**The daughter houses of Merton priory founded between 1120 and 1149**

| Date of Foundation | Location | Founded by | With | No. of Canons |
|---|---|---|---|---|
| 1120 | Taunton, Somerset | William Giffard, bishop of Winchester (1107-29) | Guy of Merton, d.16 May 1124 | 26 |
| 1121 | Plympton, Devon | William Warelwast, bishop of Exeter (1107-37) | Geoffrey d. August 1160 | 40 |
| 1123 | St Gregory, Canterbury | William Corbeil, archbishop of Canterbury (1122-36) | Alvred? | 13 |
| 1123 | Bodmin, Cornwall | William Warelwast, bishop of Exeter (1107-37) | Guy of Merton, d.16 May 1124 | 13 |
| 1128 | Holyrood, Edinburgh | David, king of Scotland (1124-53) | Alwin d.1155 | up to 25 |
| 1131 | Cirencester, Gloucestershire | Henry I, king of England (1100-35) | Serlo d.1147 | max. 40 |
| 1132 | St Lô, Normandy | Algar, bishop of Coutances (1132-51) | Theodoric | ? |
| 1135 | Dover, Kent | William Corbeil, archbishop of Canterbury (1122-36) | | failed |
| 1149 | Twinham, (Christchurch) Hants. | Baldwin de Redvers, earl of Devon (1129-1155) | Reginald | 25 |

## 8. The Monastic Day

*"Be dressed ready for service and keep your lamps burning like men waiting for their master to return ..."*
Luke 12: 35/6

The call to prayer

Today we live by the clock with the day beginning at midnight, but this was not always so. "God called the light day and the darkness night" (Gen.1:4), and from earliest times the tasks of the day were spread over the hours of daylight with the noon-day sun denoting the middle of the day. The monasteries followed the Roman reckoning of dividing each day into twelve parts or hours. Only at the equinoxes (March 20 and September 22) was the hour of 60 minutes.[123] Monasteries devoted four parts to prayer and psalmody, another four to study and private devotions and approximately four parts to manual labour to maintain self-sufficiency. Special services were performed about every three hours and were known as Prime, Terce, Sext and Nones. These together with Matins, Evensong (Vespers) and Compline constituted the seven Canonical Hours. In addition, mass was celebrated each morning and there were two minor 'offices' of Lauds and Collations at the beginning and end of the day.

Psalms constituted an important element in all services and even governed the hour for the first office. "At midnight [not by the clock], I rise to give thanks to Thee" (Psalm 119:62). Thus the brethren were roused for Matins in church, and as the church doors were locked at night, there was usually a direct passage from the dormitory into the transept of the church. Matins would be sung for almost an hour followed by a brief service called Lauds. It consisted of Psalms 148-150, a reading, a hymn (e.g. *Te Deum*), a canticle and the Lord's Prayer. Its name comes from the dominant theme of the three concluding psalms – *Laudate Dominum* (*Praise the Lord*). All brethren knew the Psalter by heart, for every psalm was sung every week.[124] After retiring once more to their beds until sunrise, the first Hour of the day was observed with Prime, followed by an early mass for certain officials. While this was being celebrated, most of the brethren would be washing and taking care "not to blow their noses with the towels, or to rub their teeth with them, or to staunch blood, or to wipe off any dirt".[125]

In the dining hall breakfast consisted of bread and ale, probably consumed standing up. This was followed by chapter mass in the lady chapel when a small bell summoned all to church before the

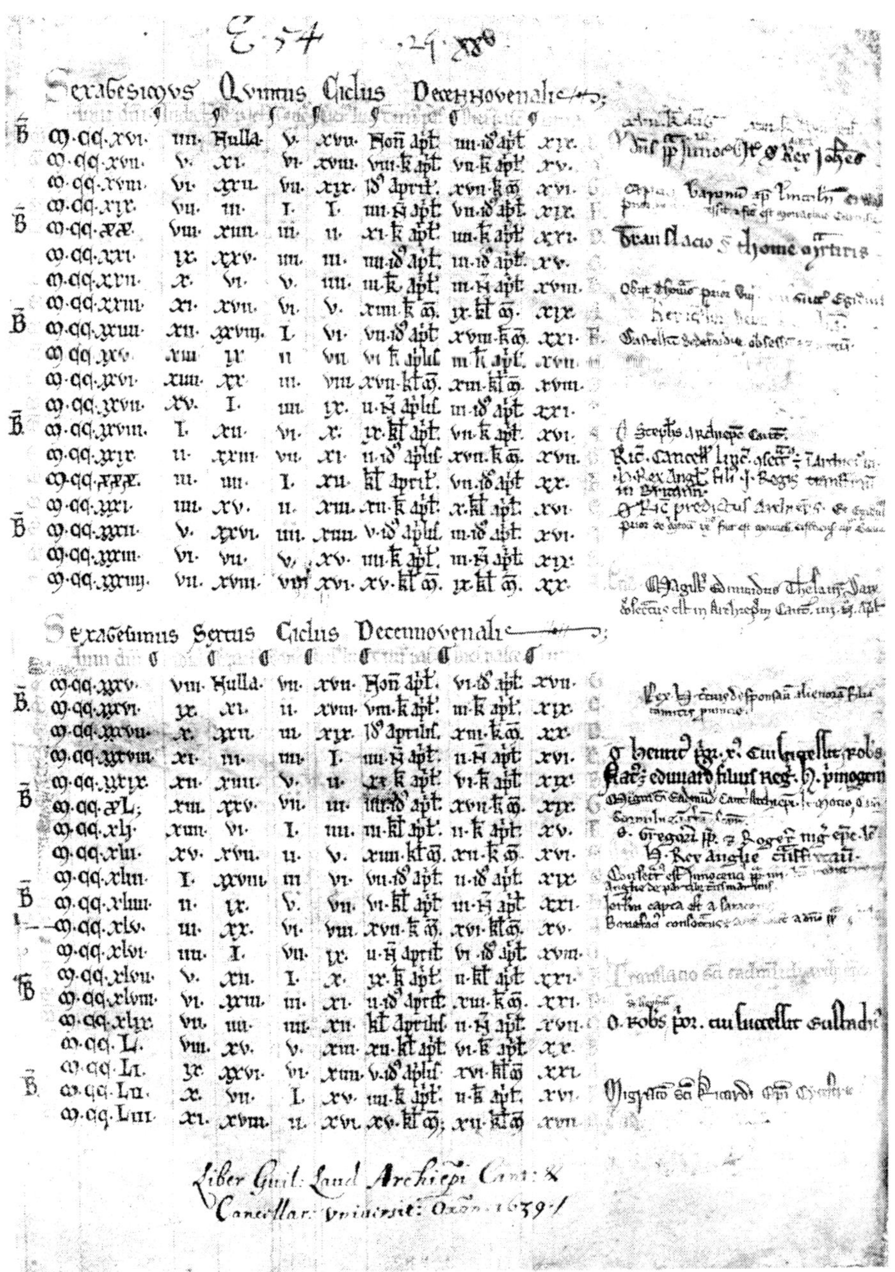

*Kalendar – Bodleian Library MS Laud Misc 723*
*The page relates to the sixth week after Easter (Sexagesima). Top heading is the 5th cycle (years 1216-1234) Lower heading is the 6th cycle (years 1235-1253). In a different script at the bottom it says: "The book of William Laud, Archbishop of Canterbury & Chancellor of the University of Oxford. 1639."*
*(Photograph reproduced from A Heales –* The Records of Merton Priory *(1898) by courtesy of the Bodleian Library, University of Oxford.)*

chapter assembly. Whilst it was ringing, the cloister had to be vacated and all stood in church and faced east until the bell ceased ringing. At the conclusion of mass, the great bell rang for the chapter meeting;[126] the novices led the procession to the chapter house to discuss business matters. At Merton the prior sat in the centre of the apse under a suspended crucifix. On either side, in order of seniority, sat the canons along the north and south walls. The central part was kept clear, revealing a floor paved with monumental slabs and brasses commemorating earlier priors.

The first part of Chapter was called *pretioso* (a precious thing – Psalm 116:15). Each day various saints were commemorated and every monastery compiled its own Kalendar of favourite saints (see illustration opposite). The relevant martyrology for the day was read, and time was allowed for house prayers. The name 'chapter' derives from a reading of a chapter of the Rule of St Augustine. Next, the necrology was read, which named members of monastic communities recently deceased. Information on the notice-board (*tabula*) was read out, which gave the names of those responsible for specified services and other duties for the day. An exhortation or sermon was then usually given by the prior and on completion he uttered the words, "Let us speak of the affairs of our house". This marked the end of the *pretioso* and all novices, lay brothers and strangers left, for it was decreed that what followed was private and no canon should discuss transactions outside Chapter.

Any new agreements or gifts were discussed. These could affect either the monastery internally or any outlying property. Any new leases, rents, tithes, presentations, dues etc. were outlined, but no agreement was binding or legal unless the consent of Chapter was given and the deed sealed with the priory seal – usually referred to as the Chapter seal.

Complaints (*clamationes*) were then heard, often concerning meals when sometimes pittances (treats) were promised. The prior then commanded, "Speak of your own order" i.e. own behaviour, whereupon any canon with a conscience stood up, came forward, confessed and asked for pardon. The *Circator*, the officer responsible for good order around the cloister, made his statement with any accusations. Any named canon left his place and stood in front of the prior, bending his knee, and waited patiently whilst complaints were preferred against him. After the accusation any other canon could support the charge or speak to the contrary. The prior then pronounced sentence and imposed penalties.

Punishment could consist of a period of fasting on bread and water, or a loss of precedence in Choir and Chapter, and even corporal punishment. The last was performed immediately in the presence of the canons with a specially provided monastic rod (*balai*). Serious misdemeanours could warrant solitary confinement, or excommunication, or expulsion from the Order. At the conclusion of Chapter, the canons changed into day shoes.

The office for the third hour was Terce sung before the high spot of each day. This was the celebration of high mass which involved rich vestments and elaborate liturgy. The high altar was appropriately decorated by the sacrist who ensured that all vestments were in good condition and vessels used in the service were clean. Acolytes carried long tapers and processions moved around the church with the asperging of various altars and claustral apartments accompanied by joyous eucharistic singing. Any important visitor staying at the priory would join the occasion – even the king (Henry III was in the habit of spending Easter at Merton). After passing around the cloister the procession entered the nave of the church and stood before the rood screen whilst an anthem was sung. A bidding prayer was said, the Lord's Prayer and prayers for the dead.

The sixth hour was Sext which was a short service, read in church before all the community adjourned to the dining hall for the main meal of the day. One sentence from a reading was completed before brethren commenced eating. The Rule of the Order specified that "at the table [they] listen to what is customarily read, without noise or protest; and use their jaws for eating only, and their ears for hearing the word of God".[127] The meal consisted of two hot dishes consumed in silence but accompanied by suitable passages uttered by a reader for their instruction in goodness. On Sundays, Tuesdays and Thursdays it was usual to have a meat dish and on other days fish, eggs and cheese.[128] After dinner the canons were allowed to sleep in the dormitory or could amuse themselves with games in the cloister.

The next office Nones was sometimes put back an hour in the long hot summer days. Then followed manual work either in the cloister copying or illuminating manuscripts, or making and repairing clothes, or making spoons, candlesticks, bee skeps etc., or teaching. Some would choose to work in the gardens or fields. After their daily work, the canons were summoned to church by a bell for Vespers (evensong). Ablutions followed before partaking of a light supper in the dining hall. This may have been served only on feast days during the winter months, and never on fast days or during the season of Lent. The minor office of Collations took place in the chapter house when the official for the week gave a short reading from Lives of the Fathers (*Collationes Patrum*).

At dusk all entered the church for Compline. This office was sung in winter with only two altar candles to relieve the darkness. At the conclusion, the canons left one by one with raised hoods. The Greater Silence (*summum silentium*)[129] began and the canons ceased all conversation, even in the parlour, until Prime the next day. The *Circator* made his final rounds, locking doors giving access to the church and cloister, extinguishing unnecessary (cresset) lights.

This concluded the day.

# 9. Administration Within

*"All who profess and call themselves Christians"*
Book of Common Prayer

This chapter deals with administration of the priory under its 'Customs and Observances' within the precinct. The prior was responsible for discipline, but many other agents outside the monastery were also involved.

The Augustinian Rule was based on a letter from the saint, addressed to a community of nuns. It was of such brevity that communities supplemented it with customaries or observances which set down regulations to guide the conduct and activities of canons. Those at Merton were used elsewhere, for around 1146, when Buckenham priory was founded, the bishop of Norwich decreed that the canons should follow in all things the established rules of the church of St Mary of Merton.[130] Three sets of books containing sermons, customs and constitutions were kept at Merton. One set was with the prior, another with the sub-prior, and a third set with the 'Master of the Order'.[131] The constitutions established the structure of internal operations.

Every professed canon took a vow of obedience to the prior, and discipline was governed in several ways. At the daily meeting in the chapter house a time was spent when all were invited to voice any errors seen in others. These were discussed and any necessary punishment immediately meted out. No brother of inferior grade could flog a senior, and no deacon could flog a priest.

## Visitations

Perhaps the most feared examination came from visits from the bishop. All Augustinian foundations were subject to episcopal visitations at intervals of roughly three years. These were performed by the bishop in person or by an official acting for him, accompanied by a legal adviser and a public notary who would write down an account of the proceedings. The visitors would be received at the west door of the priory church and proceed to the high altar with the pealing of bells and the organ playing.

All then went to the chapter house to hear an appropriate sermon and all lay folk left.

The prior produced a certificate with a list of all the brethren, and the bishop examined the prior and canons one by one, *secrete et singillatim*, in order of seniority down to the novices. The prior produced accounts for the past year, the *status domus*, and an inventory of jewels and plate. Visits were usually completed in a day. Later a report was prepared of matters requiring action (*a comperta*) which was delivered and expounded by the visitor's clerk.

On 25 September 1305 a visitation produced evidence of a lack of discipline, and prior Edmund was asked to resign. He was given a place of residence within the precinct, a companion and suitable rations.[132]

On 26 July 1314, canons were informed "that no one [should] absent himself from the Divine Offices, by day or night nor from the canonical Hours or Masses without reasonable cause and licence". They were warned not to be seen by secular persons with bows and crossbows or other things.[133]

On 27 September 1387, the canons were condemned for wearing precious furs, knotted sleeves, silk girdles, gold and silver ornaments, and for employing and keeping hunting dogs.[134] At this visitation the bishop requested that the seal of the priory be kept under five locks. Keys were to be held, one by the prior, one by the sub-prior, one by the precentor and one each by two brothers of the community.[135]

In 1492 the archbishop of Canterbury made a visitation to Merton.[136]

The evidence of the canons at the visitation of 1509 must have included much criticism of the prior, William Salynge. He was warned by the bishop not to spare needful corrections "as he had been used to do by favour for some or to oppress others undeservedly".[131] The prior was reminded of his duties and ordered "to instruct and feed the brothers with the food of holy doctrine personally twice a year in the chapter house". This doesn't seem too onerous! The canons reported to the bishop that the prior had been keeping company with women and selling jewels.[137] Canons were never invited to voice praise, only failings. (As a consequence, records of visitations can present a very distorted picture of the establishment.)

### Provincial chapters

Discipline was also ordered at provincial chapters of the Order, perhaps as early as 1207 in the York province and 1217 for Canterbury.[138] These were introduced to set standards of behaviour for all Augustinian houses to follow. From 1233 to 1341 separate chapters were held for each province. These were convened every three years and attended by the heads of all Augustinian monasteries. At each gathering two Presidents were elected, one who preached a sermon whilst the other celebrated mass. The chapter appointed two Visitors who inspected houses in their province for three years until they succeeded to the two Presidencies at the end of their term. These visitations achieved some unity for the Order but failed to change the "old and reasonable" customs of individual monasteries.[139]

The provinces proved too large an area for the Visitors to visit all houses and from 1341 England and Wales were divided into 22 areas. When the prior of Merton became Visitor he was responsible for Augustinian monasteries in the dioceses of Salisbury and Winchester.[140]

**Priors of Merton attending provincial chapter meetings**

| Year | Representative | Position | Location | Source |
|---|---|---|---|---|
| 1276 | Gilbert de Aette | President | Leicester | Salter p.xii. |
| 1318 | William de Brokesborn | President | Aldgate, London | Salter p.xiv; Heales p.220 |
| 1343 | John de Littleton | President | Northampton | Salter p.52. |
| 1346 | William Friston | President | Leicester | BL Addl MS 38665 fo.26. |
| 1362 | Geoffrey de Chaddesley | Visitor | Newstead | Salter p.xxvi. |
| 1365 | " " " | President | Barnwell | Salter p.66. |
| 1368 | " " " | Vice-president | Northampton | BL Cott.Vesp.D1 fo.57. |
| 1383 | Robert de Windsor | Visitor | Newstead | BL Cott.Vesp.D1 fo.51; Heales p.264 |
| 1386 | " " " | President | Barnwell | Salter p.77. |
| 1389 | " " " | President | Northampton | Salter p.xxix. |
| 1392 | a canon of Merton | ?Visitor | Northampton | Salter p.xxix. |
| 1395 | Michael de Kympton | (as canon) | Northampton | |
| 1443 | John Kingston | Visitor & Vice-president | Osney, Oxford | Salter p.xxxii, 104, Heales p.300. |
| 1446 | " " | ? | Northampton | Salter p.108 |
| 1503 | William Salynge | Visitor | Osney, Oxford | |
| 1506 | " " | President | Barnwell | Salter p.122; Heales p.137. |
| 1518 | " " | President | Leicester | Salter p.132, 143. |

Salter = H E Salter *Chapters of the Augustinian Canons* (Canterbury & York Society) 1922

For the Canterbury province, chapters were usually held in Leicester or Northampton as being fairly central for the majority of Augustinian houses. They were occasionally held in London but never at Merton.

It would seem that Michael de Kympton went to the Chapter meeting on 17 June 1395 and not the prior, Robert de Windsor. For failing to attend, the prior was fined £10,[141] a lot of money, and an appealing letter from the prior, addressed to the prior of Bruton (acting for Chapter), informed him that he was unable to pay his fine, pleading that "they had no small losses of cattle by pestilence, and that their dormitories and other of their old houses were ready to fall suddenly and without warning".[142]

In 1443 and 1446, prior John Kingston gave sermons in English at Oxford and Northampton.[143] For this to be recorded for posterity suggests that he was a good speaker, or that it was unusual to make an address in English. In 1506 prior William Salynge issued a mandate to the prior of St Denys, Southampton and his canons to be present in their chapter house on 19 May for his visitation, "given at his house of residence at Merton 18 April 1506".[144]

## Discipline Within

*"To the punishment of wickedness and vice"*
Book of Common Prayer[145]

Within a confined community bitter quarrels were always likely. Most dislike favouritism and canons could have petty ambitions. There was dissension in 1258 when William de Cantia tried to reform the priory and was banished.[146] William le Ferour had to leave the priory when it transpired that before he professed as canon of Merton, he had married. The bishop wrote to the prior and issued an "annulment of profession" in 1331.[147] John Paynel absconded from Merton and a visitation made by the bishop on 6 March 1335 followed the return of the 'wanderer' to his priory. The bishop asked the house to receive him back without reproach but reserved to himself the penance to be inflicted.[148] In 1347 Paynel was in further trouble having been excommunicated for attacking a servant. The bishop gave authorisation again, to absolve the canon.[149]

Punishment could involve relegation to the junior place in choir and chapter.

Sometimes Merton had to "take in" transgressors. John Cherteseye, canon of Newstead, Nottinghamshire, had been the cause of scandal "for various excesses and faults" and was sent to Merton in 1387.[150]

*One of a set of three or more broken 14th-century floor tiles, discovered from the chapter house site in 1976. These seem to be part of a chain of dancers.*
*(Reproduced by courtesy of J Scott McCracken)*

## Obedientiaries

To assist the prior in administering daily affairs, officers were appointed to oversee various departments. These were called obedientiaries. In the church there were the sacristan (church structure, vestments and plate), precentor (services) and succentor (singing and choir-school), with a custodian of the lady chapel. For food management there were the cellarer (supplies), fraterer (dining hall), and kitchener (food preparation).

All officers had servants. The sacristan had two and a boy, but one servant had to assist in gathering the harvest in August.[151]

In the hospital was the infirmarer, who cared for the sick and the retired and allowed the canons to rest after blood-letting. He was not a doctor of medicine.

The almoner provided hospitality to the needy, assisted by the guest master, whilst the chamberlain looked after clothing and bedding.

The granger had to check supplies of corn, arrange milling and issue flour to the bakehouse.

The librarian organised the scriptorium.

Other obedientiaries included the master of the works, with minor officials such as the gardener and the pittancer.

## Finance

The importance of these offices grew with the need for adequate finances, and it became the practice for income to be allocated to an obedientiary from specified property sources. In 1220 the Augustinian Provincial Chapter decreed that every house should appoint two receivers to be responsible for all priory income.[152]

As a measure of outgoings in percentage terms, the following is suggested:

| | |
|---|---|
| Feeding and clothing canons, household and guests | 30% |
| Restocking property | 20% |
| Expenses of prior and household | 15% |
| Fees to bishops and provincial chapters | 12% |
| Royal and papal subsidies | 10% |
| Payments to officials | 5% |
| General administration | 5% |
| Charitable giving | 3% |
| | 100% |

Nothing has been included for disasters, lawsuits or repaying debts.

*Excavation of the medieval mill at Merton priory 2003*
*(Reproduced by courtesy of MoLAS)*

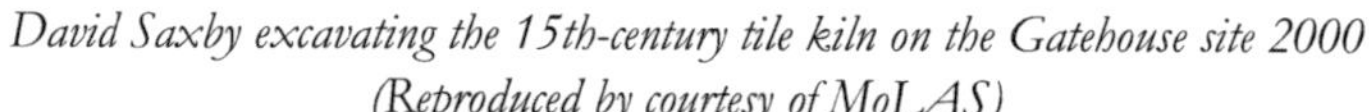

*David Saxby excavating the 15th-century tile kiln on the Gatehouse site 2000*
*(Reproduced by courtesy of MoLAS)*

# 10. Administration Without

*"I will tear down my barns and build bigger ones … And I'll say to myself 'You have plenty of good things laid up for many years'."*

Luke 12:18/19

The prior negotiated external relations and was the lord of many manors, where he had to dispense justice and maintain peace within the communities. In this he was assisted by stewards and bailiffs, some sent out from Merton and some living in the community.

An important manor given to Merton by Henry II in 1156 was Ewell. This included not only the manor itself but also the sub-manors of Kingswood (south Banstead), Shelwood (near Leigh), and Pachenesham (north Leatherhead). In the early years, lands were worked on a communal basis, with the priory's lands intermingled with lands of the community. Feudal tenants had to work certain seasonal days for the manorial lord, which gave rise to disputes and anger when the lord was not resident and never visited them.

Merton owned fisheries on the Thames at Brentford, Richmond and Eton (see page 48). These provided some of the requirements of the priory where fish was part of the diet on meatless days, although much still came from the eastern ports of England. A weir-keeper would have been resident at Merton's fisheries.

Many mills were owned by the priory and, although they were let out to tenants, the priory was involved in the maintenance of roads and bridges in order to give access to its properties and distribution of produce.

All this necessitated much travel by stewards and officers to oversee operations and safeguard priory income. In the 13th century the practice of 'high farming' began, in which smaller parcels of land worked by various people were amalgamated into bigger units. This enabled the stock on manors to be improved and increased.

Often churches were appropriated, with the bishop's permission. This gave the priory the right to the greater tithes of the parish and to employ stipendiary priests to perform duties in their churches as perpetual vicars. At the Council of Oxford in 1222 it was stipulated that the minimum stipend should be 5 marks p.a. (£3.33).[153] Where appropriated churches had farms, monasteries sometimes purchased additional land to increase tithe income. Where the vicar had a fixed income this could result in proportionately less for the vicar, and new agreements were negotiated to compensate. For a list of appropriated churches see page 76.

Prosperity came in the early 14$^{th}$ century, when continued benefactions enabled churches to be rebuilt and farms re-ordered. Larger barns were required for increased amounts of produce. Land improvements included drainage and the long-term planting of oak forests. Roads and bridges were improved to assist trade. Monasteries were now part-religious and part-economic, alongside lay owners and the commercial interests of towns like London. Farming policy and estate management affected towns as much as the countryside.

In 1346 England was enjoying the best of times and the king was celebrating victories in Europe with theatricals at Merton (see Chapter 13 – Royal Visitors). One hopes that the priory used increased opportunities for the relief of poverty, sickness and senility.

The life of opulence resulting from sound estate management suddenly came to an end in 1348 when the Black Death made its appearance. This scourge created a shortage of labourers, and land owners found it beneficial to let animals graze instead of men working the soil and in some areas sheep rearing took over.

## Granges

*"Weeded and worn the ancient thatch*
*Upon the lonely moated grange"*
Lord Tennyson *Mariana*

When a monastery owned farms and manors fairly close together but at a distance from the mother house, administration was best achieved by setting up a miniature monastic house in the area. It was the Cistercians who first built large barns to store produce before transporting home. The Norman word for 'barn' was *grange* and this name was adopted for the new settlement.

A grange farm would consist of a large barn and other buildings set around a courtyard. On one side were the domestic quarters, hall with kitchen and often, at one end, a chapel. It was approached through a gatehouse and within the precinct were the stables, fishpond and gardens, if possible with a stream. Two canons and perhaps a bailiff were responsible for its operation, and they hired labourers as necessary. To avoid transport difficulties it was preferable to sell produce locally apart from seed and feed.

Throughout the medieval period the Thames valley was a major supplier of food for London, with the river itself facilitating the conveyance of goods to the capital. Merton priory was one of many monasteries that set up granges in the county of Buckinghamshire. With the gradual abandonment of demesne farming in the late 14$^{th}$ century, many granges were leased out to tenants.

### Amerden grange

This was a moated site near Bray lock on the Buckinghamshire side of the Thames. In 1197 Merton priory was granted 92 acres (17 ha) of land and the right of assart, the clearance of woods for tilling. The Bray Court Rolls refer to *bournhames eyte* in 1361 in connection with the grange. Burnham Abbey was close by and Merton probably provided food for the nunnery.

### Upton grange

This was a large establishment in Buckinghamshire, complete with chapel (now St Laurence church).

After Henry VI founded Eton college in 1440 he wished to bestow property along the Thames upon the college. On 8 June 1443 Merton priory was required to grant Eton certain land and fisheries in the manor of Upton, and on 8 February 1444 the tithes of the manor of Upton and a further dyke were added.[154] The importance of Upton Grange must have diminished thereafter.

The main building still exists, and has been known since the Dissolution as The Grange. A newspaper proprietor purchased the building in the 1970s and has saved and restored one of Merton's medieval treasures.

*Upton Grange – August 1991 (photograph by the author)*

### Eton grange

This was a sub-manor of Upton and probably used the barns and other buildings. there. In 1301 Edward I borrowed £50 from Merton priory and the amount was secured from sales at its granges. Eton sold over 200 quarters (2.54 tonnes) of corn, lavender, beans and peas.[155]

Included with these granges were Thames fisheries and islands from Taplow and Amerden downstream to Eton (Bullokeslok).

### Tregony grange

The grange furthest from Merton was Tregony in Cornwall. This had been a priory and came into the possession of Merton in 1267 when an exchange was made for the church of Cahagnes, Normandy.[156] Conventual life proved difficult and on 26 April 1282 the bishop of Exeter agreed that the priory should become a grange staffed by a single canon. One wonders if this was treated as a respite duty or as transportation punishment. At that period Tregony was a port with access to the river Fal.

### Kingston grange

The vicar's grange at Kingston was near the parish church but was out of use by the end of the 15th century. The churchwardens' accounts for 1503 refer to "a vacant plot of land where the grange had stood". A large barn was located on the site now occupied by the railway station.

## Granges in Merton

Many of Merton's granges were not distant centres; in fact two moated sites were within the parish of Merton. Instead of housing resident canons both were leased out in the 14th century.

### West Barnes grange

This was situated in the valley of the Beverley Brook on the western boundary of the parish. Its large barns survived until the 20th century. In 1536 it included "all buildings, barns, stables and gardens ... of 30 acres" (12 ha),[157] and lands totalling 579 acres (234ha).

*West Barnes Farm, by Cyril Wright, from W H Chamberlain* Reminiscences of Old Merton *(1925)*

### Grange farm

This was situated outside the priory precinct to the west, and was in existence before 1178.[158] A large barn was associated with it which in 1753 measured 78ft x 22ft.(23.8m x 6.7m).

## Finance

Monasteries provided a safe-deposit, and hence served as bankers for important persons.

**Income** in monastic terms was described as arising from Spiritualities or Temporalities.

SPIRITUALITIES came from churches, and could emanate from incumbents who had been presented to the living by the priory. This was an annual payment termed a "pension". A major source of income came from the tithes of appropriated churches. Rights of presentation were saleable properties[159] and some monasteries sold indulgences – although there is no mention of these in known records of Merton priory.

TEMPORALITIES came from tenants who worked priory lands or lived in priory property and from manorial mills which charged tenants for grinding their corn. Demesne farms were worked by monastic servants and the income from sales of grain, wool, timber etc. would be treated as trade, as was income from fisheries.

Other income arose from perquisites from manorial courts (fines etc.), benefactions, loans from Jews etc., and sale of corrodies (see Chapter 12 – Hospitality).

## Outgoings

The two largest items were repair of buildings and the cost of lawsuits which could arise from encroachments, trespass, ownership and financial disputes. Subsidies were regularly paid to crown and pope, and there were travel costs, including journeys to Rome, and highway responsibilities.

The expenditure accounts for property still exist for the ten years 1383-1392:-

| | Lands & Tenements Acquired | Purchase of stock | Repair of Buildings | Total |
|---|---|---|---|---|
| | £ | £ | £ | £ |
| 1383 | | 29 | 563 | 592 |
| 1384 | | 33 | 71 | 104 |
| 1385 | | 10 | 28 | 38 |
| 1386 | | 21 | 57 | 78 |
| 1387 | 9 | 66 | 245 | 320 |
| 1388 | | 3 | 186 | 189 |
| 1389 | | 2 | 35 | 37 |
| 1390 | 41 | 12 | 56 | 109 |
| 1391 | | 121 | 61 | 182 |
| 1392 | | 43 | 140 | 183 |

Source: Bodleian Oxford . Laud. MS 723 Fol. 101. Figures rounded to nearest pound.

The total income for 1392 was £897 and the outgoings £984, resulting in a net loss of £87.[160]

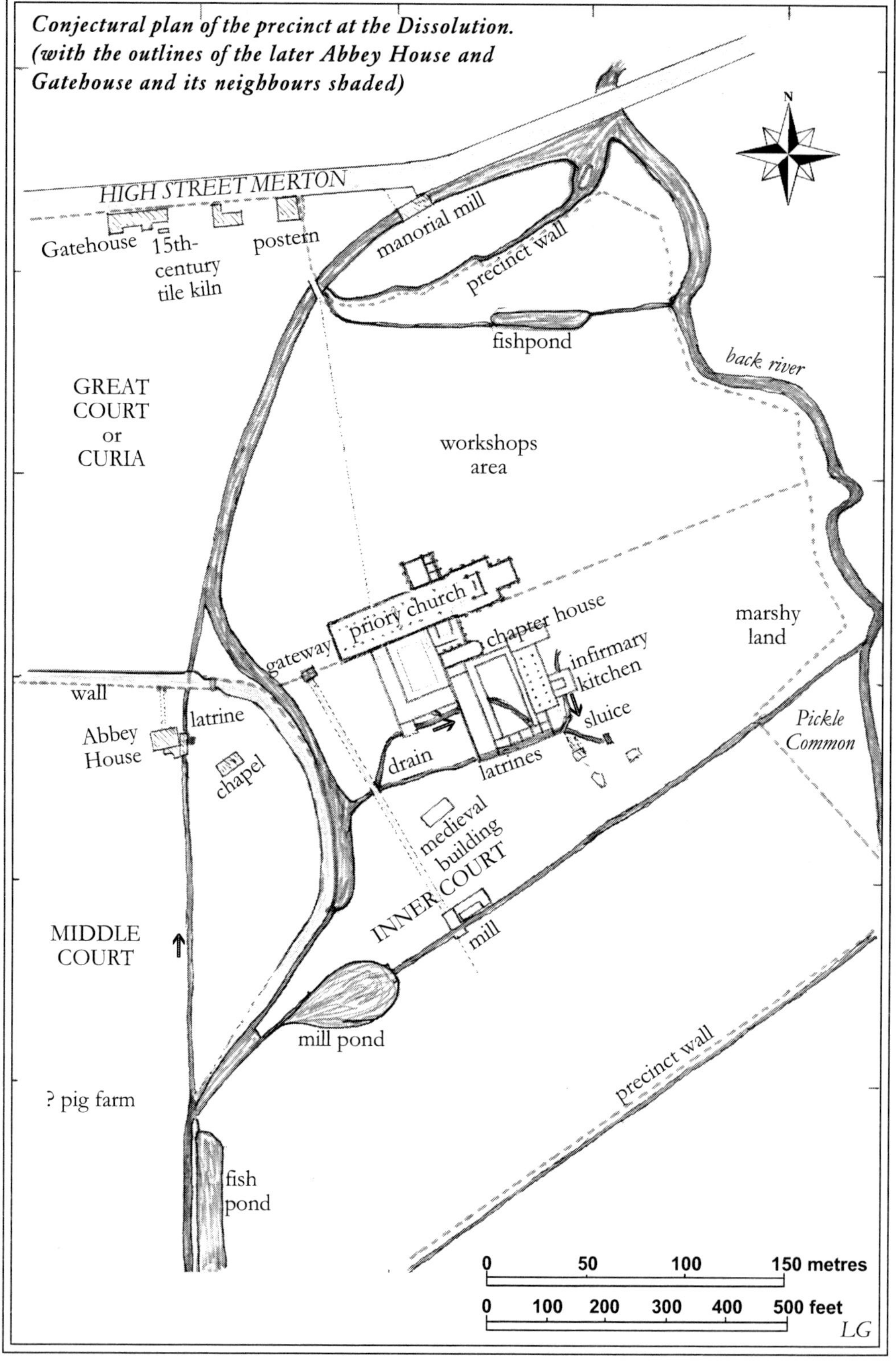
Conjectural plan of the precinct at the Dissolution.
(with the outlines of the later Abbey House and
Gatehouse and its neighbours shaded)
N
HIGH STREET MERTON
Gatehouse
15th-
century
tile kiln
postern
manorial mill
precinct wall
fishpond
back river
GREAT
COURT
or
CURIA
workshops
area
priory church
chapter house
infirmary
kitchen
sluice
marshy
land
gateway
wall
latrine
Abbey
House
chapel
drain
latrines
Pickle
Common
medieval
building
INNER COURT
mill
MIDDLE
COURT
mill pond
? pig farm
precinct wall
fish
pond
0 50 100 150 metres
0 100 200 300 400 500 feet
LG

# 11. The Precinct

*"City of God, how broad and far*
*Outspread thy walls sublime!"*
Dr Johnson *A Hymn*

Merton priory was enlarged in Henry II's reign and again in the reign of Henry III. The precinct rapidly filled with a variety of buildings. The total extent was about 65 acres (26 ha) – a large monastery by any standards.

It was surrounded by an 8-ft (2.44m) high precinct wall built of flint, and in length some 1½ miles (2.5 km), with a moat outside the wall except perhaps along the High Street where buildings would have provided adequate security. The wall prevented the entry of vagabonds, lessened noises from without, and restrained temptations to leave the precinct.

The presence of the River Wandle was an important factor in the choice of the site. The river had earlier flowed further to the east and marked the parish boundary between Merton and Mitcham, but the main flow was diverted by the priory to pass through the centre of the precinct. This provided water for filling fishponds, washing and waste disposal, driving mill-wheels, supplying the moat, watering gardens and orchards.

Around the south-eastern and eastern sides, a residual stream called 'the back river' or 'the pickle ditch' followed what had been the main channel of the river in Saxon times. In the period 1200-1250 other ditches were cut both inside and outside the precinct wall in the north-eastern corner.[161]

The precinct was divided into courtyards, each serving a specific function. Thus there were areas set aside for prayer, study, food preparation, eating, recreation, sleeping, hospitality, workshops and storage. Besides the Great Court, there was a Middle Court for private individuals and an Inner Court where all domestic activities of the priory were carried out, and where building and repair work took place. Around the claustral area were rooms and buildings set aside for administrative purposes and the maintenance of worship, discipline and instruction. The courts gave access to other zones, and it was usual for them to be separated by walls and inner gateways. Parts of the precinct were reserved for recreational use, with gardens, orchards, vines, herbarium and fishponds. Areas prone to flood, both within and outside the precinct, were reserved as water meadows and marshlands. These lands would also provide homes for waterfowl such as ducks, swans and geese. In the early days a farm may have been situated in the south-west corner of the precinct, but during the period of 'high farming', 1250-1345, cereals were produced at the granges and the precinct no doubt had a pig farm. The use of bran from the bakehouse, malt dregs from the brewhouse, together with the kitchen waste, enabled pigs to convert waste into protein for the good of the community.[162]

The location of buildings was dictated by various factors, including the availability of water and liturgical practice. The priory church was built on the best site – the highest firmest ground and north of the river. Adjoining it were the claustral buildings, orientated to enable the midday sun to warm the north walk of the cloister, with the church providing shelter from the north winds. On the south side of the cloister were the dining hall and washing place (*laver*), and on the east side the chapter house with dormitory adjoining above. The cloister was an open court, enclosed by covered alleys or walks which served specific purposes. The north side was for work and reading and the west was used for learning and for teaching the novices.

It is impossible to describe all the changes to buildings in the precinct over four centuries, but the majority took place in the latter half of the 12th century and the second quarter of the 13th, although new building took place in every generation. The undertaking of "new work" made heavy demands on a monastery, necessitating the procurement of building stone, timber, iron and nails, lead, sand, chalk, canvas, glass, oil etc., and the engagement of masons, carpenters, painters, glaziers and labourers.[163] So much monastic building was taking place in the 13th century in England, creating a mountain of debt, that the papal legates Otto (1237) and Ottoboni (1267) ordered that no existing building could be demolished without licence from the bishop. Fortunately, Merton had its own stone-quarry at Chaldon, Surrey. It is only possible here to mention a few changes to some of the buildings.

## The Great Court

This was the hub of all the activities of the priory, and at Merton was referred to as the *Curia*.[164] Everyone passed through the Great Court at some time. Here guests were received, messengers and servants came and went. There was an imposing gateway (the *Magna Porta*) with the porter's lodge attached which allowed admittance. The Augustinians made a great display with their gatehouses and many were later enlarged to become architectural features of some magnificence. At most monasteries there were at least three phases of construction and many were rebuilt in the 14th century.[165] There was an opening high enough to allow loaded wagons to pass through as well as a side gate for pedestrians. The location of Merton's gatehouse is not known but it would have given access to the Great Court. Major Heales included a plan of the priory in his *Records of Merton Priory* in 1898 which marked the gatehouse at the corner of Abbey Road and the High Street. A building called Gatehouse existed in the High Street, east of that site, until 1906 but excavations on its site have been inconclusive as to its original use.[166]

Once the visitor had passed through the gatehouse the vista of the priory church would have loomed ahead, with its west front and the central tower dominating the skyline.[167] Visiting dignitaries would enter by the west door for an impressive procession to the high altar before conducting business.

*Above*
*Southern elevation of Gatehouse (postcard of c.1900, reproduced by courtesy of J Goodman)*

*Could the double archway be medieval in origin?*

*Below*
*Excavations at Gatehouse site in 2000 (photograph reproduced by courtesy of MoLAS)*

*Above*
*Gatehouse – the north elevation abutting Merton High Street (postcard postmarked 1905, reproduced by courtesy of J Goodman)*

Adjoining the gatehouse was the almonry where the almoner had his lodgings (*domus elemosinarium*). Each day, baskets of unused food from the dining hall were sent to the almoner to aid the poor and sick. The almoner also housed wayfarers and taught in the song-school.

The bakehouse (*pistrinum*) and the brewhouse (*bracinum*) were probably located in the Great Court. Bread and ale were important commodities in every monastery, as they were used for almsgiving as well as for sustenance of the brethren and guests. The sacrist was responsible for providing unleavened bread used at mass but this was often made in a special oven within the church. Another reason for the bakehouse to be located in the Great Court was to encourage villagers to use the manorial ovens. The cellarer was the master brewer and involved in producing ale of quality. The brewhouse was close to the malting kiln and contained vats for steeping and draining the barley.

Domestic buildings, such as the tailor's shop (*sartrinum*), storehouses, other lodgings and the communal stables, were situated in the Great Court. A smithy was on hand for shoeing and making nails, hinges, locks etc.

In the middle, away from buildings, was the pigeon-house or dovecote (*columbarium*). These constructions were introduced by the Normans and were used to supply young birds (squabs) for the table for unexpected guests. Only feudal lords and religious houses were permitted to have dovecotes.

There may have been another gateway giving direct access from Grange farm to the granary and kitchen area such as that provided at Waltham.[168] This would not have been ornamental and could have been situated where Abbey Road now meets High Path.

Some buildings had more than one use. Towards the end of the 13th century, prior Gilbert de Aette (1283-92) built a chamber *juxta Beaulieu*. When prior Edward de Herierd resigned in 1305 he occupied this building.[169] In 1336 the house of the almoner and Beaulieu were together large enough to accommodate a meeting for the whole community.[170]

Special guests passed through to an Inner Court via another gateway. Anyone wishing to visit a canon was escorted to the outer parlour or guest parlour in the west range of the cloister, where the visitor waited. This was an imposing room built in the style of the period, with stone benches on each side.[171]

## INNER COURT – CLAUSTRAL BUILDINGS

**The Church –** Unlike in Cistercian houses there was great variety in the layout of Augustinian buildings. A long nave was a feature for local lay folk, with easy access, avoiding the claustral area. Spaciousness in the nave suggests a wish to cater for large congregations. There was the parish church in Merton village, but many lived and worked close to the priory and would have used the priory church. There was a lay cemetery north of the priory church.

The walls of the church were plastered and painted, sometimes decorated with designs copied from manuscripts. Windows were filled with painted glass. Glazed floor tiles were laid in the transepts and in the processional area of the central nave. In the aisles of the nave was paving from Reigate stone quarries. To reduce draughts in lofty churches and to provide privacy for the canons, a *pulpitum* was erected to the east of the choir screen.

An important part of a church during the later Middle Ages was the **Lady chapel**. An altar, dedicated to St Mary, existed in the first church at Merton,[172] but this was probably the high altar. By 1200 the cult of the veneration of the Virgin was systematised in the western Church, and special chapels were built for her in cathedrals and most monasteries.[173] At Merton, a "new chapel of St Mary" was built in the reign of Henry III,[174] rebuilt 1320-50, and needing repairs in 1393.[175] It included Purbeck 'marble' columns from Dorset. In the 15th century a custodian was appointed to be responsible for the upkeep of this chapel.[176]

*Merton priory – floor of the nave – north side, looking west – 1988*
*(photograph by the author by permission of the site director)*

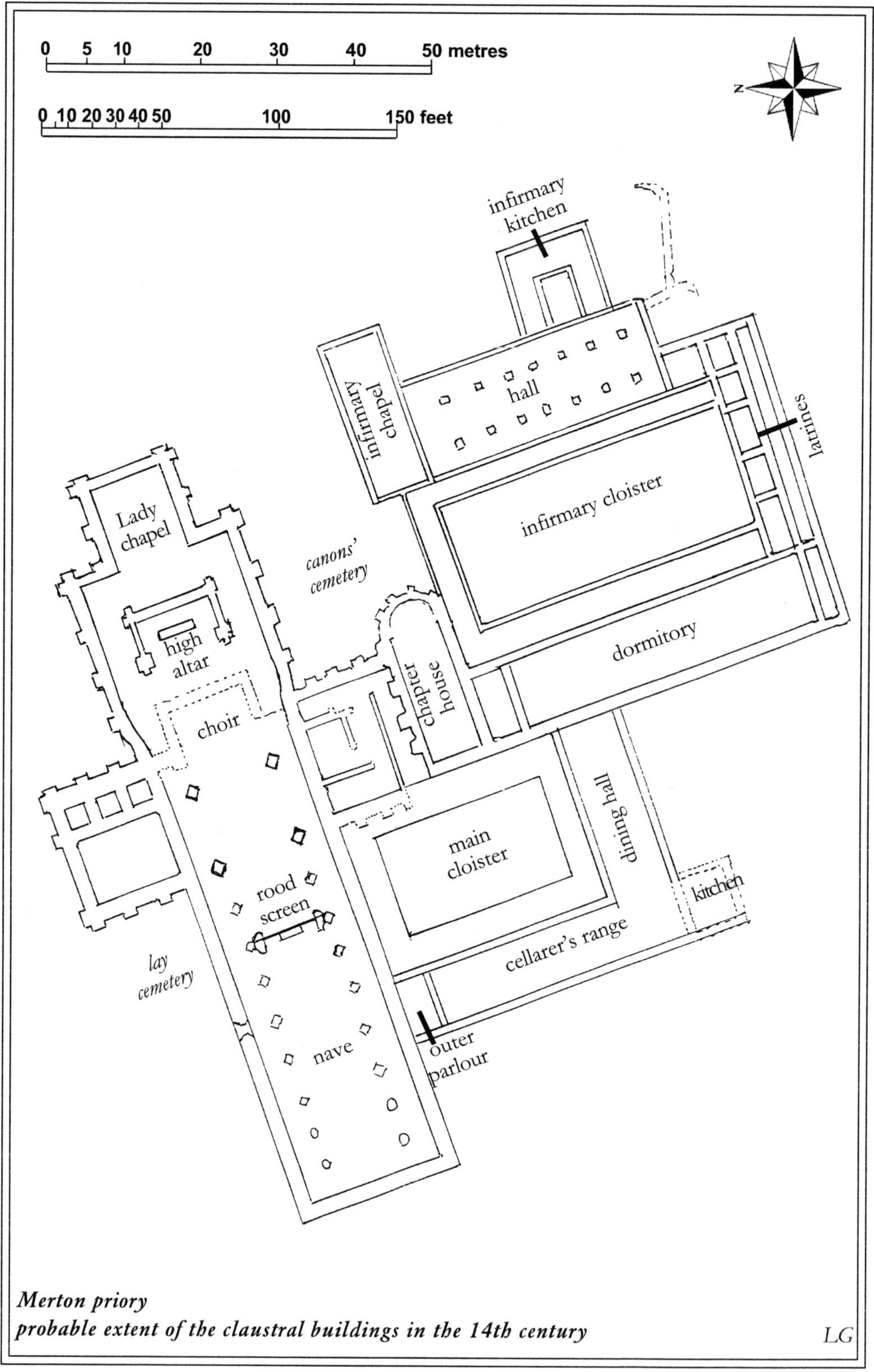


***Merton priory***
***probable extent of the claustral buildings in the 14th century***

**Chapter house (*capitolium*) –** The canons met each day in the chapter house to discuss and transact the business of the monastery. The entrance would have been highly decorated and an eastern apse was added to enhance the building and to provide more light with additional windows.

*The chapter house excavations in 1978. (Photograph reproduced by courtesy of J Scott McCracken and Surrey Archaeological Society)*

It was a sacred building and here the priors were laid to rest. Excavations have revealed 33 graves. In one grave near the west end of the chapter house, two coins minted at York were found which date from 1473 and 1476. The prior at this time was John Kingston, the 27th prior, who held the post for 44 years, from 1442, and who must have been a great age when he died on 2 January 1485. In 1471 the bishop allowed him special privileges.[177]

*Plan of burials in the chapter house (reproduced by courtesy of MoLAS)*

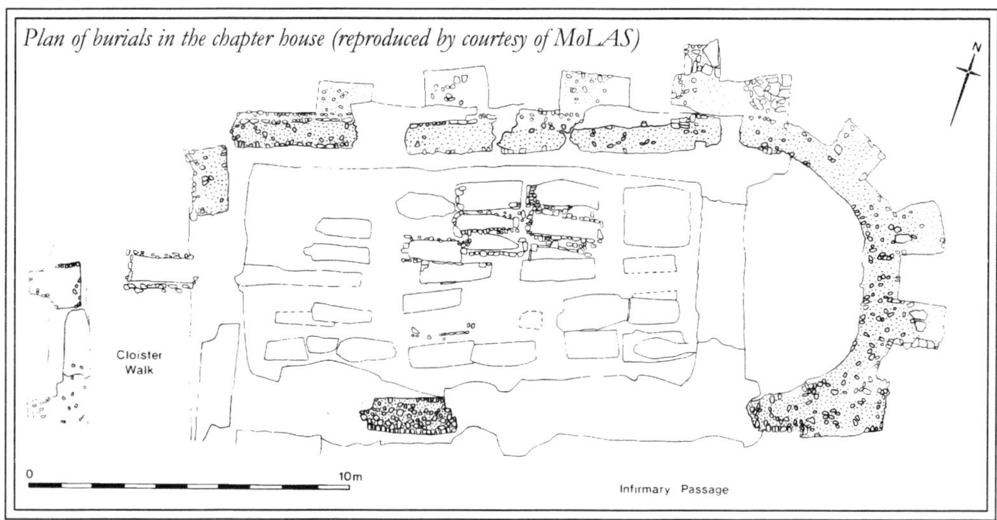


**Prior's lodging –** In the early days of the monastery, the prior would have slept in the dormitory with the other canons and eaten in the dining hall. But it soon became necessary for the prior to have separate lodgings in the west range of the cloister to entertain visitors.

As more manors or estates were granted to the monastery, the prior became a feudal magnate with a large establishment including his chaplain, valet, stewards, cook, porter and watchman. His importance was such that the prior's revenues were separated from those of the priory. He now required a separate set of buildings, a 'house of residence' (see page 42) which would have been magnificent, a fine example of small-scale domestic architecture.[178] Rooms and windows were of ample size, with probably an oriel window added in the 14th century. Together with the garderobe it possibly had wash-basins fed by taps from a cistern. Ceilings and fireplaces would have been lavishly decorated, and the walls covered with painted cloth or a tapestry. The prior no doubt maintained his own chapel. Even the smallest monastery provided comfortable quarters for the superior.[179]

There is evidence that at Augustinian monasteries the prior's lodging was often situated at the south end of the west range.[180] At Merton the prior retained a room near the cloister for in 1530 when a new prior-elect had been nominated, the elect retired "to a certain inner chamber commonly called the prior's chamber".[181]

**King's Chamber** – Large monasteries were used by the king on his progresses around the country. Quite a few were royal foundations like Merton, and the king would exercise founder's right of lodging. Rooms, normally part of the prior's lodging, were reserved for royal use and maintained at the king's expense. Buildings at Merton also accommodated the king's chancellor.

At Durham was a "goodly brave place, much like unto the body of a church with very fine pillars on either side, and in the middle of the hall a large fireplace. The chambers in it were richly furnished, especially one called the king's chamber".[182]

On 1 December 1257 the king ordered the royal mason, John of Gloucester, to repair the chimney of the king's chamber at Merton "and of his garderobe, and of the king's chancellor's chamber there."[183]

**Dormitory (*dorter*)** – This was at first-floor level having two staircases, one descending directly into the church transept to enable canons to attend Matins at midnight. The other stair communicated with the cloister. Each canon had an allotted space in the dormitory and slept on a straw pallet. The area was divided into cubicles in the 14th century to offer more privacy for the canons.

**Latrines (*rere-dorter* or *necessarium*)** – These were situated at the south end of the dormitory and consisted of a two-storied building of considerable size and well ventilated. The main drain, a stone-lined channel, passed beneath. Sluices were situated near a garden for ease of access when enriching the soil with manure.

**Cellarer's range (*cellarium*)** – This was normally on the west side of the cloister below the prior's lodging. In the 15th century the cellarer had a first-floor chamber near the dormitory.[184]

**Dining Hall (*frater*)** – This was always aligned east-west and usually situated above the level of the cloister, with cellarage space below. In a side wall was a pulpit from which portions of pious works were read during meals.

**Writing Room (*scriptorium*) and Library –** These were situated in the cloister in the early days, with books and manuscripts contained in aumbries (cupboards), built into the inner wall of the cloister. The brethren wrote and illuminated manuscripts in the north walk. Study-cubicles were often provided, known as 'carrels', containing a desk with writing materials. Carrels were originated by Augustinian canons in 1232.[185] Later a room was sometimes built above the cloister walk. There are plenty of signs that Merton priory possessed scribes of considerable industry.[186]

**Kitchen (*coquina*) –** At the west end of the dining hall was the kitchen which was often partly detached with a stone roof because of fire risks. On the roof was a lantern with louvred panels to allow easy dissipation of steam and cooking smells. Other buildings were provided to support the work in the kitchen – the buttery (for storing drink), pantry (for storing food), and the bolting-house for sifting flour.[187]

Further away was the butchery and tannery. Offensive, smelly or noisy undertakings – beast slaughtering, leather preparation, etc. – were kept well away from the claustral or daily working areas. There were also corn barns (*granaria*), the grain dryer, ox-house and cow-house.

**Infirmary (*infirmitorium*) –** The Augustinian Rule stressed the importance of adequate food, shelter and medical care, although this was only available for the religious. The works of mercy for outsiders rested with the almoner.

Merton's infirmary was situated south-east of the claustral buildings, secluded and furthest away from the bustle of the Great Court. The main building was a spacious infirmary hall, and the infirmary cloister separated it from the dormitory range. Access was from the infirmary passage south of the chapter house, much used, and excavations have revealed that the floor was re-laid on at least 15 occasions. The hall served for rest, exercise and for meals. It was aligned north to south and excavations have revealed a food preparation area where fruit was a predominant feature. The Observances of Barnwell expected that the infirmarer be always prepared. "It should rarely or never happen that he has not ginger, cinnamon, peony and the like, ready in his cupboard, so as to be able to render prompt assistance to the sick if stricken by a sudden malady …".[188]

A larger hall was built about 1225 with a central hearth for some comfort in cold weather. The hearth consisted of roof tiles on edge and set in mortar. The roof was supported by two rows of piers to form aisles. The floors were covered with roof tiles.

Beds were laid along the aisles against the walls. Later the aisles received partitions to form rows of cubicles.

Blood letting was performed on canons eight times a year, for mental, physical and spiritual stimulation. A vein was cut to release 'bad' blood to restore the balance of the humours (blood, yellow bile, black bile and phlegm). It was considered a treat as canons could rest in the infirmary or physic garden for three days enjoying better food and the comfort of a fire in winter.

To the east of the hall were the infirmarer's lodging and the kitchen. The infirmary chapel was probably a building north of the hall.

*Hearth from one of the partitioned rooms in the infirmary (photograph by W J Rudd by permission of the site director)*

With all the claustral and ancillary buildings, this zone extended south to the mill (see plan page 50).

### Middle Court

**The Guest-house –** This would be sited away from the Great Court and the claustral buildings, so that the comings and goings of guests did not interfere with the canons' duties. In charge of the guest-house was the *hostillarius* who supplied fresh rushes for the floors and attended to the needs of important guests. The cellarer was required to visit on occasions "to see that there is neither waste nor deficiency there".[189]

When the priory was enlarged about 1165, a separate building for important guests was built. This would have consisted of a hall, latrines, meat-kitchen, parlour and a chapel – all probably on two floors. A channel of water was drawn off the main flow of the Wandle to service the kitchen and latrines before continuing northward to join another flow which supplied a second mill. A courtyard with separate stables would have been provided, and in 1312 the king's sergeant stayed with royal horses. Edward I paid £20 for the expense of horses and the wages of the grooms.[190]

An ancient building known in later years as Abbey House was demolished in 1914. A Norman archway was revealed which had been incorporated into the front door-case, and may have been part of the guest-house. The arch has been reconstructed beside Merton parish church, but the site of the house is now covered by a road, Merantun Way, and waste land. The design of the doorway has been dated to about 1175.[191]

*The arch discovered within Abbey House when it was demolished in 1914 (Reproduced by courtesy of Merton Library and Heritage Service and the Wimbledon Society)*

*The arch as reconstructed near St Mary's Merton Park in 1935 (Reproduced by courtesy of Merton Library and Heritage Service and the Wimbledon Society)*

*Watercolour c.1830 showing the rear of Abbey House and the mill serving the calico works, founded in 1724 (Reproduced by courtesy of Merton Library and Heritage Service)*

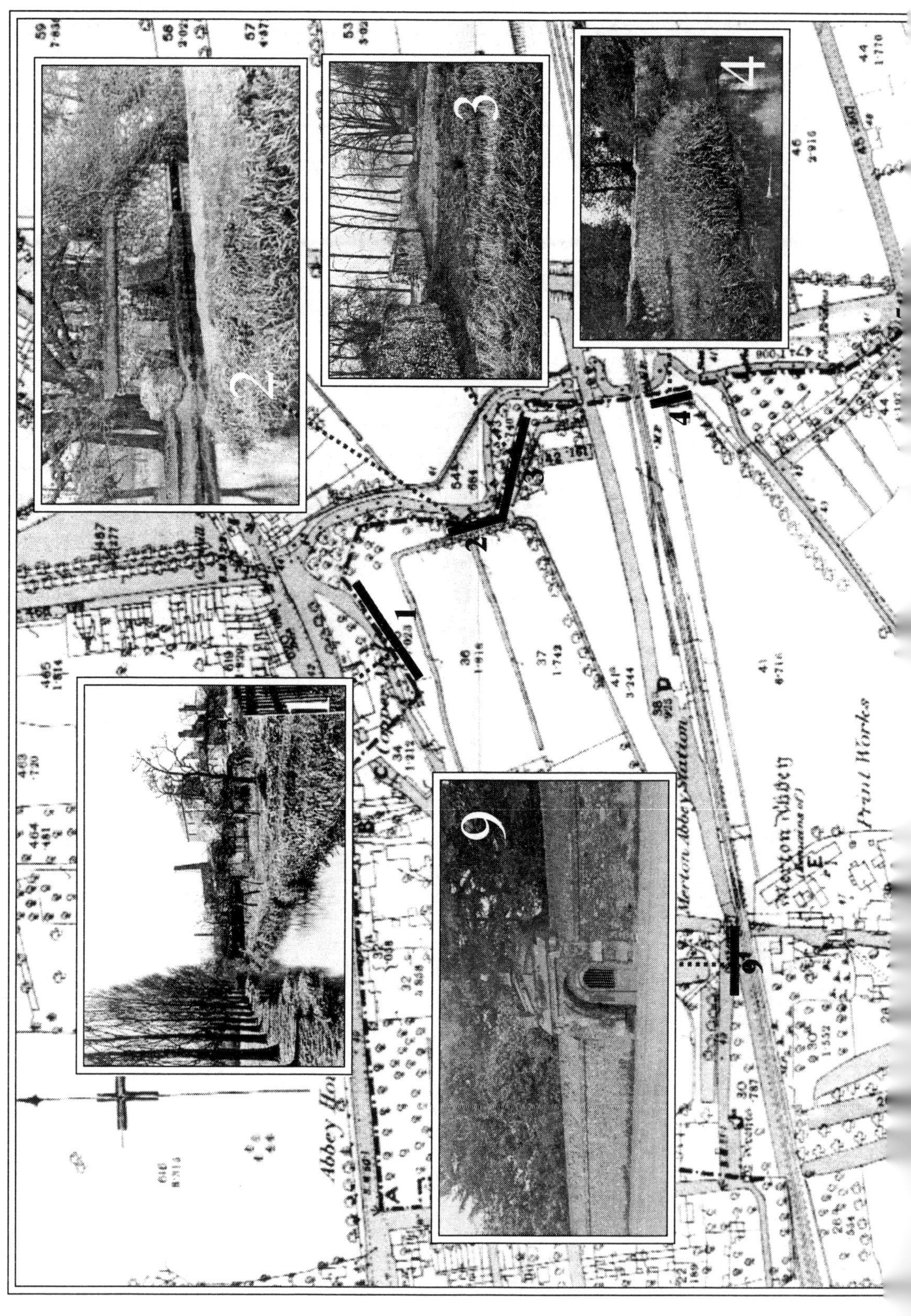
Merton Abbey Station
Merton Abbey
Print Works

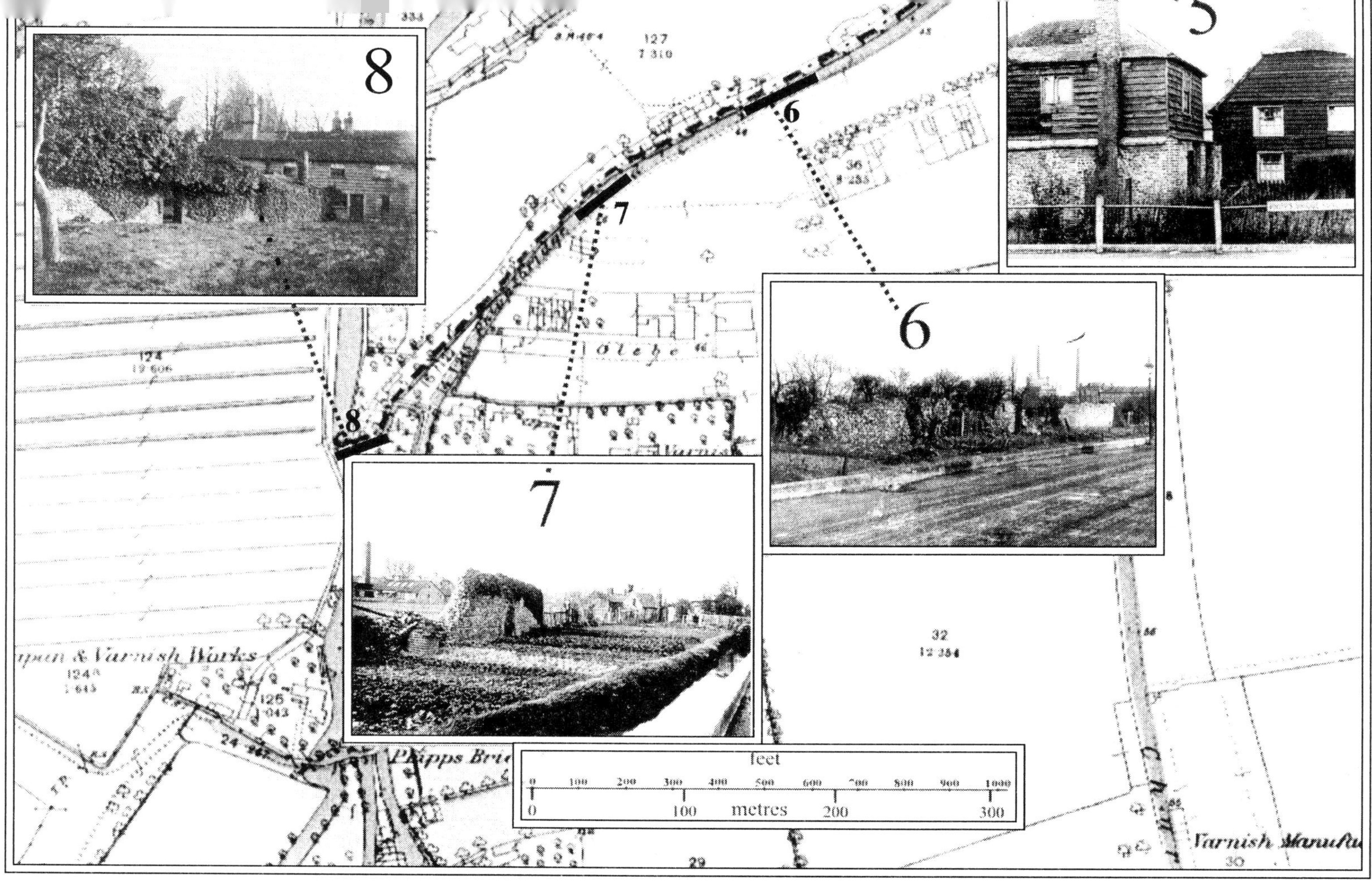


*Early 20th-century photographs of the surviving sections of the priory wall, superimposed on an extract from the 1870s edition of the 25-inch Ordnance Survey map.*
*(Photographs 1-7 copyright Wimbledon Society, photographs 8- 9 copyright Merton Library and Heritage Service. Reproduced by permission. This arrangement by Cyril Maidment)*

## Inner Court II

This was situated north of the presbytery of the church and contained the workshops, but at a distance because of fire risk. The stone masons' lodge and yard was here, as was the blacksmith, tinsmith, plumber and glazier. Most monasteries had their own tile kiln, not only for making tiles for precinct buildings but also for other property. By early in the 14th century, itinerant tile makers caused monastic kilns to pass out of use. Merton decided to reintroduce tile making and built a new kiln about 1480 near the High Street, to produce roof tiles, probably for repairs to the church, infirmary and reredorter. This kiln was constructed of re-used late 12th century Reigate stone.[192]

*Tile kiln discovered during excavation of the Gatehouse site 2000 (photograph reproduced by courtesy of MoLAS)*

Large monasteries also had a bell furnace, but no evidence has been found at Merton.

**Cemeteries –** Canons were buried to the east of the chapter house, some in wooden coffins, sometimes within a stone-lined grave, and at times in a shroud. The lay cemetery was north of the church and most of those interred were buried in cloth shrouds (see also Death of a canon on pages 22 and 24).

**Use of the river –** The main flow of the river passed to the south of the Inner Court which contained the site of the monastic mill. Attached to the mill was an oven which may have been a drying room, and a large late medieval stone-lined tank, possibly used in the manufacture of parchment. The mill was rebuilt in the 16th century when a new head-race was constructed with re-used Reigate stone.[193]

Further south, but still within the precinct, were "two or three fishponds which communicated with the river close by …".[194] These were necessary for easy access to fish, and for breeding and storing fish. Flood meadows would have been set aside to take excess waters.

**Other Gateways –** Workers from Merton, Mitcham, Morden and Tooting would have been employed at the priory and additional gateways and posterns gave access to the precinct. In 1240 there is reference to a gateway "near the crossroad to Carshalton".[195]

**Other buildings –** There were many lodgings in the precinct to house the hundred or so corrodians, monastic servants and their families. These are referred to many times in the records, for example in 1216, 1225, 1301 and 1305, with one residence built between the sacristy and the House of Chaplains in 1286.[196]

## 12. Hospitality

*"You did it for me ..."*
Matthew 25:40

Many important people stayed at Merton. Ewan, bishop of Evreux in Normandy, adopted the habit of a canon of Merton in 1139. His brother Thurstan, archbishop of York (1114-40), wished to resign in favour of Ewan "who was ranked amongst the most learned men of his day". But Ewan died before a decision had been reached by pope Innocent II and he was buried at Merton.

When Hubert Walter was elected archbishop of Canterbury in 1193, he followed Becket's example (see Chapter 16) and came to Merton, adopting the dress of a canon of Merton.

Merton's hospitality extended to two canonised sons, Thomas Becket and Edmund Rich. Edmund was born in the year of the martyrdom of Becket and lived close to Becket's birthplace on the north side of Poultry in the City. Edmund had intended to teach theology, but the schools at Oxford were closed in 1209 following a town versus gown dispute after the hanging of two clerks. In addition the pope was in dispute with king John and had laid an interdict[197] on England from 1208 until 1214, although this was ignored in the diocese of Winchester (and also Norwich). Edmund chose to spend a year or more in retreat at Merton 1213/4 preparing for his lectures until the schools of Oxford reopened in the autumn of 1214.

It was probably while Edmund was living at Merton that on 1 August 1213 archbishop Stephen Langton came to Merton to resolve the problem of the interdict with the bishops of Ely, Lincoln and London.

The fact that Edmund chose this place for his retreat suffices to convince us that its reputation at that period stood very high for strict observance of religious discipline. It was Edmund's favourite resort, not only on that occasion, but subsequently as archbishop, when "he would often leave his occupations and go there to refresh his spirit with the exercises of religious life".[198]

*Consecration of St Edmund Rich by Roger le Noir, bishop of London 2 April 1234*
*Based on British Library MS Roy 14C vii*
*Matthew Paris* Historia

Edmund was consecrated archbishop of Canterbury on 2 April 1234, and was back at the priory in 1236 presiding over the Council of Merton (see Chapter 16). In 1239 he held an ordination in the priory church, and he returned in 1240 and died soon after.[199] Merton priory petitioned the pope to make Edmund Rich a saint, informing him that he spent time at Merton "going in and out as one of the canons themselves". Edmund was made a saint in 1248.

Hubert de Burgh arrived for a different reason. He was Justiciar (virtually the prime minister) and came in 1232, but found it necessary to seek sanctuary. The pope had accused him of withholding revenue of the churches in England which were held by papal nominees. He was hated by Londoners for hanging the leader of a popular riot, and the king charged him with mismanaging treasury funds. He was summoned to attend a council at Lambeth but refused to leave the safety of the priory. The king ordered the mayor of London to raise all citizens who could bear arms and take him dead or alive. As many as 20,000 men set out for Merton brandishing arms and waving banners. When de Burgh was informed he prostrated himself before the high altar. The earl of Chester warned the king of the danger of the mob and he revoked the order, much to the disappointment of the crowd. Hubert de Burgh left Merton to seek sanctuary elsewhere.

*'Hubert de Burgh, barefoot and clad only in his undergarments, before the altar of Merton, awaits in prayer his death. For the citizens of London, his enemies, are approaching.' Based on a drawing by Matthew Paris in his* Historia, *now in the British Library*

In 1263 William Vadlet sought refuge having committed a murder, and Henry de Michelham for stealing a chalice.[200]

Bishop Bronescombe was fond of staying at Merton. In 1257 he was archdeacon of Surrey and was made bishop of Exeter in 1258. He returned to Merton on 15 March 1258, and came again on 25 March 1260. His final visit was on 23 January 1280 and he returned to Exeter where he died on 22 July 1280.[201]

John Peckham, another archbishop of Canterbury, loved visiting Merton and died at the priory on 8 December 1292.[202] From 1270 to 1277 he was a lecturer at Oxford and in 1278/9 at Rome. Pope Nicholas III appointed him to be archbishop and, although this was against Peckham's wishes, he was enthroned at Canterbury on 8 October 1279. He invited the prior of Merton to attend.[203] The archbishop defended church authority, which upset the king and nobles and resulted in the passing of the Statute of Mortmain. This prevented a dying person from giving land to a church or corporation. Such gifts could not be sold or transferred, as it was in a dead hand (French – *mortmain* = dead hand). The statute was designed to curb the increasing wealth of the Church and safeguard feudal dues. Peckham corrected many abuses of the Church and in 1281 tried to check the growth of plurality (the holding of more than one benefice at the same time).

He enjoyed the hospitality of the priory on 2 November 1281[204] and wrote to Rome in 1282 commending Merton as "the best of the religious in his Province".[205] In April 1282 he had to invoke a threat of excommunication (to be excluded from communion and privileges of the Church) against William Daumbeses for being hostile and disturbing the liberties of Merton priory.[206] The archbishop came to Merton again in 1292, died later that year, and was buried at Canterbury near the martyrdom site of Thomas Becket on 19 December.

William of Wykeham was chancellor (twice) and became bishop of Winchester in 1367. He helped to set up the Good Parliament which passed laws to regulate trade and protect subjects from oppression. John of Gaunt returned to England after fighting in France, and dissolved Parliament. He decided to reduce the power of the bishops and replaced several prelates (including Wykeham) with barons in parliament in order to reverse the measures previously passed. Wykeham was accused of embezzlement of a million pounds and of releasing French hostages for bribes. He was forbidden to come within 20 miles of the royal court and left Southwark Palace in December 1376 and sought refuge at Merton priory. He was probably reminded that Merton was only eight miles from Westminster and he moved on to Newark priory which was 23 miles from London. No doubt he wished to be at his palace at Farnham but feared the consequences, as he was no longer bishop. Instead in January/ February 1377 he went to Waverley abbey. In June 1377 Richard II came to the throne and Wykeham was pardoned. He then endowed a college at Winchester and founded New College, Oxford in 1379.

In June/July 1526 Edward Seymour, duke of Somerset and later Protector of England stayed at the priory with his retinue. The cost for the wine required for his stay at Durham Place, London and at Merton priory in 1526 was £20 for three tuns (756 gallons, approximately 3400 litres).[207]

## *Ad Succurrendum*

It was the practice in the 12th century for men to enter a monastery late in life, or simply to wear the holy habit in order that they might be found thus on Judgment Day. These were known as the religious *ad succurrendum* (towards succour/salvation).

A generous grant of property accompanied the gesture and in return the donor received a canon's allowance of food and drink together with a small money allowance. Some of Merton's benefactions came from such persons, e.g. Eudo de Malden (Malden/Chessington churches) and Peter de Tolworth (Long Ditton church).[208]

## Corrodies

The practice of *ad succurrendum* became far less common from 1200 when monasteries began to grant corrodies with a legal commitment. Because this required approval of the brethren with the priory seal, the cartulary contains many records. In return for a lump sum or property, the priory undertook to provide, for the rest of the corrodians' lives, lodging, food, drink, fire-wood, candles and often clothing and

| **Lay persons giving a benefaction** | | | **page nos in Heales** |
|---|---|---|---|
| 1219 | Alice Velet | dowry land | 78 |
| c1220 | Peter Normannia | land in London | 77 |
| 1217 | Richard le Franceis and wife | | 73/4 |
| 1222x31 | Warin, merchant | | 83/4, 94 |
| 1231x38 | Sir Michael, merchant | | 94 |
| 1239 | Godiva le Viel | 10 acres of land in Mitcham | CRR XVI 871 |
| 1239x40 | Richard Besant | | 102 |
| 1239x48 | Andrew de Shelwode and wife | | 103 |
| 1246 | William de Southwark and wife | a messuage | 113 |
| 1249x63 | John de Awelton | | 115 |
| 1249x63 | Sir G de Haremede' | | 118 |
| 1249x63 | Sir John & Lady Gundreda Hansard | land of La Legh and Tolworth | 119/120 |
| c1258 | Roger le Furbur | tenement given in 1260 | 120 & 137 |
| 1264 | Jordan de Wahull | | 141/2 |
| 1288 | Andrew son of William Morel | 20 shillings(£1) | 170 |
| 1301 | Richard de Wolcherehaw and wife | | 189 |
| 1392 | un-named | 145 marks (£97) | 284 |
| c1395 | Nicholas Vyleys, grocer | | 289 |
| c1395 | John Curaunt | | 289 |

x = *limit of possible date*

*This is not a complete list of corrodians. Corrodies were also granted to priests awaiting appointment to a benefice, and as a favour on behalf of influential prelates.*

| **Superannuated servants of the crown** | | **Source** | **page nos in Heales** |
|---|---|---|---|
| 1262x72 | Hugh 'portario' | | 139 |
| 1313 | Lambert Clay | Close Roll 6 Edw. II m15. 211; *VCH* 2 p.97 | |
| 1317 | Alan de Santo Botolphe | Close Roll 10 Edw. II m5d. 219; *VCH* 2 p.97 | |
| 1318 | Geoffrey de Thorpe | Close Roll 12Edw. II m19d. 222 | |
| 1331 | Thos. Holbode and John de Bul | Close Roll 5 Edw. III; *VCH* 2 p.97 | |
| 1340 | Bartholomew de Langele | *VCH* 2 p.97 | |
| | In 1340/1 the prior denied that the king had any rights. | | |
| | In 1392 he complained of the corrody system. (Heales p.245 & 277) | | |
| 1342 | John Nichol | *VCH* 2 p.97/8 | |
| 1343 | John Mareys | *VCH* 2 p.97/8 | |
| c1377 | Edmund Tettesworth | | 264 |
| 1387 | John Mandelyn and wife | | 264,277 |
| 1400 | John ffraunceys (but prior complained Mandelyn's wife still in occupation) | | 293/4 |
| 1477 | William Clifton | Patent Rolls 16 Edward IV p.14 | |
| 1516 | Launcelot Lisle | | 322 |
| 1520 | John Westwode (pension) | Record Office Cal. | 326 |
| 1521 | John Pate, groom of the wardrobe | Record Office Cal. | 329 |
| 1530 | Sir Bryan Case (pension) | Record Office Cal. | 334 |
| **Servants of the priory** | | | |
| 1222x31 | Geoffrey de Mara (or Mora) | | 82 |
| 1222x31 | R Tapevil | | 83 |
| 1231x38 | Philip | | 94 |
| 1232x38 | Robert de Bocland and wife | | 94 |
| 1239x48 | Roger Walens | | 104 |
| 1239x48 | John de la Haye and wife | | 104 |
| 1249x63 | Gilbert de Coocham | | 121 |
| 1249x63 | William de Chesham | | 121 |
| 1282 | William de Faith, gatekeeper | | 164 |
| 1286 | Dyonisius de Thorrok Master, clerk (d.1317) | | 168 |
| 1305 | Edmund de Herierd, former prior | | 194 |
| 1310 | Henry Hoclegh, gatekeeper | | 204 |
| 1313 | Richard de Pennark | | 211/2 |
| 1318 | Geoffrey de Whethamsted | | 220 |
| 1323 | Richard Bavel | | 225 |
| **Chaplains servicing chantries** | | | |
| 1238 | Alan de Chelsham | | 102 |
| 1239x48 | Roger | | 103 |
| 1249x63 | Richard de Bandon | | 118 |
| 1307/8 | William de Colecester | | 199 |
| 1320 | John Purnel de Burgh | (for Sir Alan de Chelsham) | 223 |
| c1320 | William Gavel | | 223/4 |

forage for a horse. In 1288 Andrew, son of William Morel, bought a corrody (*corredium*) for 20 shillings (£1) but it was not extinguished for another 29 years.[209]

Corrodians were usually wealthy laymen who were received as paying guests in return for an adequate capital sum. This often was an opportunity to obtain ready money for the monastery to complete a building project or pay for repairs. In 1392 Merton sold one corrody for 145 marks (£97) when they needed 240 marks (£160) to repair the lady chapel.[210] At the Augustinian house of Kirkham, Yorkshire, the canons were in debt following the rebuilding of their choir in the 13th century. The sale of 16 corrodies met their immediate needs. In 1387 the bishop of Winchester warned the canons of St Thomas's hospital, Southwark, that they had arranged too many corrodies so that "the poor were deprived of their rightful maintenance". The scheme was an early form of pension provision, but it operated without the advice of actuaries, so often the results were financially ruinous, as the total costs exceeded the value of the capital gift.

Deeds were drawn up setting out in detail the terms and location of residence. In 1216 Sir Amicius was granted a site in the precinct "in which he had built houses which were consumed by fire".[211] In 1286 Dyonisius de Thorrok was given leave to build a house on a site near the sacristy, of 74ft x 66ft (22.6m x 20.1m).[212] This he enjoyed until his death in 1317 after 31 years. In 1310 Henry Hoclegh was given residence beside the Great Gate.[213] Between 1200 and 1350 several corrodians had their lodgings in the Curia or Great Court, some with gardens. These were probably situated along Merton High Street facing south. Corrodians were normally housed in the infirmary or infirmary cloister. There were five corrodians in the priory in 1393.[210]

Some corrodies were annuities where the priory paid a pension. Others were for food and fuel without residence. A corrody at Dunstable included the support of two boys, one of whom was at school.[214]

Hospitality without corrodies was available to lawyers, physicians, schoolmasters, and craftsmen who had served the priory. Servants were often granted a bread and beer allowance as part of their remuneration.

Royal foundations (and kings often claimed that Merton was one) gave the Crown the right to grant corrodies to ex-officers of the royal household. This included men-at-arms who had grown old in fighting for the king and became non-paying guests living on hallowed ground. In the 14th century the prior of Merton complained to the king about the system, but it was not until the 16th century that the Crown began to pay for these corrodies.

Some English kings decided to impose a royal servant **in exchange** for sanctioning the nomination of any new prior. Edward III imposed corrodians on the priory in 1335 and 1339 on the appointment of new priors. The king took the prior to court in

1341 for not admitting Nicholas de la Garderobe to a corrody at the king's command, and John Nichol was admitted in 1342. He died soon after and the corrody passed to John Mareys.[215] In 1520 Merton was required by Henry VIII to give hospitality to the minister of the chapel-royal (John Westwode) and again in 1530 to Bryan Case, in return for authorising new priors.[216]

The usual daily allowance was the convent miche (loaves), one gallon of the best beer,[217] and the current ration of food from the kitchen.[218] The corrodians were usually lay people and such generosity must have been galling to professed canons.

## Hunting

Hunting was strictly forbidden by canon law to those in monasteries, and most of Surrey was reserved for the king's pleasure under forest law. The canons were however permitted to hunt when acting as hosts to visiting dignitaries. In 1252 Henry III allowed Merton to hunt game in their manors of Surrey and Buckinghamshire.[219] A rabbit warren of 24 acres (10 ha) existed at Merton Grange. The canons were ordered not to hunt with dogs or even keep sporting dogs by themselves or others, openly or secretly within the priory or without, contrary to the Order in chapter.[220] The bishop forbade canons "to go out in sight of secular persons with bows and crossbows".[133]

*Hunting scenes on tile fragments found at Merton priory by Colonel Bidder SAC 38 pt I (1929) p.58 (reproduced by permission)*

For the prior it was a different matter. He had to maintain his position in society and in 1291 the king gave him licence to assart (remove woodland) and impark (fence in) 40 acres (16 ha) of land adjoining his estate of Northwood and Le Frith at Kingswood.[221] The prior already held a deer park at Godmanchester, Huntingdonshire. The king also requested his seneschal (steward) of royal forests in Hampshire not to annoy the prior of Merton on account of hunting with dogs.[222]

Beasts of warren included hare, rabbit, badger, pheasant, partridge and woodcock. Beasts of the chase included deer, fox and wolf.

## Bishop's Visitation

See Chapter 9 – Administration Within.

Visitors' accommodation depended on their social status. Ordinary folk and attendants would be accommodated by the almoner, close to the Great Gate. Nobles would stay at the guest-house and favoured guests might stay with the prior. Houses existed for specified officers and there was a house for chaplains of chantries associated with the priory.

*Two views of the monastic drain, uncovered in March 1990.*
*Both views look north. The latrine drain is shown in the upper photograph.*
*(Photographs by the author by permission of the site director)*

## 13. Royal Visitors

*"Come in the evening; come in the morning;*
*Come when expected, or come without warning."*
An Irish Welcome

Even before the first buildings at Merton were completed, queen Matilda (Maud), wife of **Henry I**, came to visit the site to show interest in the welfare of the monastery. This was probably in 1116, some years after she had assisted in the Augustinian foundation of Aldgate priory in London in 1107. She returned to the new site at Merton in early 1118, this time with her son, prince William, to show the results of pious deeds.[223] Unfortunately she died on 1 May 1118 and prince William was drowned in 1120 when the *White Ship* foundered. The priory mourned both deaths.

It is doubtful if **Henry II** (1154-89) ever visited the priory because he spent two-thirds of his reign out of England. But he was made aware of its presence subsequently by his chancellor, Thomas Becket, once a student at Merton. Many of the king's gifts to Merton priory were at the instigation of Becket. The charters were executed by the king and witnessed by Thomas at Caen, Rouen and Bruges in 1156 or early 1157.[224] The king gave the manor of Ewell which included the sub-manors of Kingswood, Shelwood and north Leatherhead. He completed the rebuilding of the priory and endowed it in 1165.[225]

**King John** often stayed at the priory. In 1204 he stayed from 14 to 18 June, together with the archbishop, the bishops of Ely, Salisbury and Norwich, the earl marshal and the earls of Arundel and Essex.[226] John stayed again on 8 June 1215 whilst the barons occupied London. From Merton he issued safe-conduct passes to enable a joint meeting to take place at Runnymede.[227] The king had deposited some of the royal treasure at Merton, which Adam the cellarer had to take to Winchester on 27 June 1216.[228] The king died in October 1216.

*Henry III, from his tomb in Westminster abbey*

No king of England stayed at the priory more than **Henry III**. From an early age he was involved with national events at Merton and from 1227 chose to maintain lodgings at the priory. Rooms were also set aside for the chancery so that governmental business could operate from Merton. Henry was glad to remove himself from the constraints of court life at Westminster and would often spend Christmas and Easter at Merton. He first came to Merton when only nine whilst the pope's legate, Gualo, and the regent, William Marshal, brokered a deal with Louis the dauphin of France. Following the agreement the dauphin left Merton for France in 1217.[229]

In January 1236, Henry married Eleanor of Provence and spent a week at Merton presiding over the council of Merton.[230] (see Chapter 16). While at Merton in April 1246 he prohibited a joust planned to take place at Guildford.[231] Throughout Henry III's reign many charters were attested at Merton, as follows:

| **Cal. Pat. Rolls** | **Cal. Lib. Rolls** | **Close Rolls** | **Other** | **Other Sources** |
|---|---|---|---|---|
| *(Patent = open, not sealed)* | *(Liberate = delivered)* | *(Close=sealed)* | | |
| | May/June 1227 | | | |
| | 1229/30 | | | |
| Mar. 1233 | | Mar. 1233 | | |
| Jan. 1236 | | | | |
| | 1237 | 1237 | | |
| April 1237 | | | | |
| | April 1239 | | | |
| Dec. 1245 | | | | |
| Jan. 1246 | | | | |
| April 1246 | | | | |
| May 1249 | | | | |
| May 1252 | | | May 1252 | Heales p.124 |
| | | Feb. 1253 | | Heales p.125 |
| | Jan. 1255 | April 1255 | | Heales p.130 |
| | April 1256 | Jan. 1256 | | Heales p.131 |
| Sept. 1256 | | | | Heales p.131 |
| | | | Dec. 1256 | W Kennett *Parochial Antiquities* 1695 p.251; *Mon Ang* p.66. |
| | Jan. 1257 | Jan. 1257 | Jan. 1257 | Heales p.131 |
| | May 1257 | May 1257 | May 1257 | Beds. Historic. Records Soc. xliii (1963) No. 49 |
| | Jan. 1258 | Jan. 1258 | | |
| | April 1258 | April 1258 | | |
| | Jan. 1259 | | | |
| | March 1259 | | | |
| | April 1259 | April 1259 | | Heales p.136 |
| | Oct. 1259 | | Oct. 1259 | WAM 15999d |

**Edward I** and Eleanor of Castile were crowned together at Westminster on 19 August 1274 when their young son Henry, heir to the throne, was only six years old. Henry became very ill and his mother and grandmother considered a break in the countryside would be beneficial. They stayed at Guildford palace (castle) but on the return journey they stopped at Merton where the lad died on 14 October 1274.[232] Masses were said for his soul and the cortège proceeded to Westminster for the funeral.

Edward I and **Edward II** chose to use monasteries as a source of revenue to fight their wars against certain barons, the Welsh, or the Scots, and never came to Merton for spiritual refreshment. Queen Isabella finally despaired of Edward II's way of life and visited the prior of Merton in January 1327 to seek his support in parliament to force the king to abdicate.[233]

**Edward III** was a successful king and at Epiphany 1347 decided to hold royal sports and theatricals at Merton priory.[234] He wished to celebrate his victories at Sluys (1340) and Crécy (1346). Here, 26 mummers disguised themselves with masks, as dragons and men "with diadems". Such entertainment gave rise to mockery, rooted in pre-Christian beliefs which Christianity never entirely eradicated. So the prior and convent are unlikely to have enjoyed the celebrations.

*Mummers wearing animal masks dance to music provided by a boy playing a cittern (based on Bodleian Library, Oxford, Ms. 264, f.21v)*

**Henry IV** chose to hold a privy council at Merton in 1412.[235]

The troublesome reign of **Henry VI** involved his being crowned in England and France several times. On the occasion of his 16th birthday he was crowned at Merton priory on 1 November 1437,[236] when he was given increased powers to govern England.

Princess Mary, daughter of **Henry VIII**, stayed at the priory from 17 to 19 October 1533.[237]

*A choice of crowns*
*Henry VI from a print after the painting on glass at King's College, Cambridge*

## Churches appropriated to Merton priory in the 12th century

| Place | Advowson granted | Date appropriation begun | completed | Source |
|---|---|---|---|---|
| BEDFORDSHIRE | | | | |
| Bedford - St Peter | | | | |
| Eaton Bray with Whipsnade | *c.*1130 | *c.*1130 | 1211 | |
| BUCKINGHAMSHIRE | | | | |
| Upton | before 1157 | | | |
| CAMBRIDGESHIRE | | | | |
| Barton | *c.*1174 | 1267 | | Heales p.147 |
| DORSETSHIRE | | | | |
| Coomb Keynes with Wool | *c.*1171 | *c.*1171 | 1291 | Heales p.74 |
| East Lulworth | *c.*1220 | 1338 | | Heales p.74 |
| HAMPSHIRE | | | | |
| Bishops Sutton with Ropley | *c.*1170 | *c.*1172 | 1340 | Heales p.25 |
| HERTFORDSHIRE | | | | |
| Kimpton | *c.*1200 | *c.*1220 | | Heales p.65 |
| Stanstead Abbots | *c.*1160 | before 1190 | before 1291 | Heales p.45 |
| HUNTINGDONSHIRE | | | | |
| Alconbury | before 1274 | | | Heales p.155 |
| Godmanchester | *c.*1140 | 1218 | | Heales p.74/5 |
| KENT | | | | |
| Patrixbourne with Bridge | before 1198 | 1258 | 1399 | Heales pp.45/6,292 |
| Ryarsh | | 1242 | | Heales pp.110,132 |
| NORTHAMPTONSHIRE | | | | |
| Flore | *c.*1200 | 1200 | | Heales p.55 |
| OXFORDSHIRE | | | | |
| Duns Tewe | *c.*1120 | *c.*1120 | | Heales pp.27,35/6,297 |
| SOMERSETSHIRE | | | | |
| Midsomer Norton | 1174x87 | *c.*1212 | 1292/3 | Heales pp.26,43,179 |
| SURREY | | | | |
| Carshalton | before 1148 | *c.*1180 | 1297 | Heales pp.26/7,47,261 |
| Cuddington | 1121x30 | 1186 | 1309 | Heales pp.39,166,202 |
| Effingham | *c.*1147 | *c.*1180 | 1299 | Heales.p.178 |
| Kingston, with the chapels of Thames Ditton, E Molesey and Sheen. (Petersham had its own endowment for a chaplain) | "from a very early date" | | *c.*1160 | Heales p.66, 67 |
| Merton | before 1121 | before 1121 | | |
| WILTSHIRE | | | | |
| Somerford Keynes | *c.*1174 | *c.*1174 | 1338 | Heales p.74 |

x = limit of possible date

# 14. Endowments

*"...the one who has been entrusted with much, much more will be asked."*
*Luke 12: 48*

The barons and knights who supported the Conqueror in 1066 were rewarded with properties scattered across many counties of England. By the time Henry I became king, a succeeding generation possessed these diffused estates and found them difficult to administer. Many of the less convenient properties were given to endow religious houses. This often made sense, as the monasteries could take a long-term view of their economy and improve land, clearing wastes and woodlands. As this coincided with the growth of the Augustinian Order, monasteries' endowments were spread widely.

Gilbert the founder of Merton was not one of the nobles. He was one of Henry I's 'new men', those "of ignoble stock and raised, so to speak, from dust, and exalted above counts and illustrious castellans ...", or so wrote a contemporary English monk Orderic Vital[238] who spent his life in Normandy. But Gilbert was instrumental in obtaining endowments from sons of noblemen to support his new foundation. Barnwell possessed many churches from its foundation.[239] (See p.7) Gilbert was able to persuade the king to convey the minster church of Kingston to him.[240] This church also served East Molesey, Thames Ditton, Petersham and Sheen (Richmond). It may have been in the mind of Gilbert that the priory would become a centre for administering and satisfying all spiritual demands of endowed parish churches.

After the king's gift of the manor of Merton to the priory in 1121, Robert the prior "sent word to bishops, abbots and others about the poverty of the institution. Each gave what he could, and some nobles, upon entering Merton contributed certain things ...".[241] Hugo, brother of the prior, gave the church of Tew (Duns Tewe), Oxfordshire "which was a great means of support".[241]

Gisulf the Scribe was drowned in the *White Ship* disaster in 1120. His successor was Bernard who, with his brother, spent much time re-establishing family fortunes which had been lost. As they retrieved property between 1120 and 1130 it was entrusted to Merton priory. His brother eventually became a canon at Merton. Hugh de Lavel gave the church of Cuddington to Bernard, and this together with the church of Kingscliffe, Northamptonshire, came to Merton.[242]

About 1147 William de Dammerton granted to the priory the church of Effingham,[243] and Faramus of Boulogne gave the church of Carshalton. Also in the 12th century William Testard gave the churches of St Mary and Holy Trinity at Guildford. The advowson of Ewhurst church was also given to the priory.

About 1150, the priory was granted the church of King's Norton, Somerset.[244]

To add to the churches around Kingston; Malden and Chessington were given to the priory by Eudo de Malden, and Long Ditton by Peter de Talworth,[245] although not until about 1185. Eudo's father, William, had given a hide of land in Malden about 1150.[246]

## Appropriated churches *(see table on p.76)*

The normal process by which monasteries received income from a church was by appropriation when the religious house became the 'rector' of the parish. Perpetual vicars were appointed to perform parochial duties and were paid a stipend to cover costs. After appropriation some incumbents retained the tithes but paid a pension to the monastery, whilst others took only the lesser tithes and received some payment from the monastery. The approval of bishop, king and pope had to be obtained for appropriation, which often took years.

Of the 289 appropriated churches in the diocese of Winchester, the Augustinian houses held 53 churches, of which Merton priory held 10.

## Manors

When Henry II granted the manor of Ewell to Merton priory in 1156 it marked a change in feudalism. Ewell manor was the economic and judicial centre for many of the priory's smaller estates in the neighbourhood, some of which became independent manors in due course. With the granting of other estates throughout England, the prior became responsible for the repair of highways, the upkeep of bridges, clearing ditches and obstructed pathways, polluted mills and many other obligations. In each manor the prior employed bailiffs and stewards to act for him and administer the manorial courts.

By 1242 there were 200 estates in 16 counties. In 1535 Merton was receiving income from 69 churches, 35 manors and 39 mills. In Surrey, Merton owned 24 manors and had an interest in 15 mills. Of the churches in Surrey, eight had been appropriated and Merton held the advowsons of another six.

*Part of the surviving precinct wall, looking west, 1990 (photograph by the author)*

| County | Manors | Mills |
|---|---|---|
| Buckinghamshire | Taplow | Taplow (3) |
| | Upton including Wexham | |
| Devonshire | Canonteign | |
| Dorset | Winterbourne Stickland | Bere Regis |
| | | Bradford |
| Hampshire | Holdshot | Holdshot (fulling) |
| | | Mattingley |
| Hertfordshire | Morehall (Thorley) | Stanstead Abbots |
| Huntingdonshire | | Huntingdon |
| Kent | Patrixbourne | Dover |
| | | Greenwich |
| | | Lullingstone |
| | | St Paul's Cray |
| Middlesex | Charlton (Sunbury) | Charlton |
| Norfolk | | Blickling |
| | | Castle Acre |
| | | King's Lynn |
| | | Salthouse |
| Northamptonshire | | Flore |
| Oxfordshire | Milcombe | Somerton |
| | | South Weston |
| Somersetshire | Midsomer Norton | |
| Staffordshire | Calwich | |
| Surrey | Little Ashtead | Carshalton (2 + fulling) |
| | Banstead (*c.*1377) | East Molesey |
| | Berwell (Kingston) | Ewell |
| | Biggin & Tamworth (Mitcham) | Fetcham – 'La Hale' |
| | Cannon Court (Fetcham) | Kingston – Middle |
| | Chessington at Hook (Kingston) | Merton – Amery |
| | Coombe Nevill (Kingston) | Priory |
| | Dunsford (Wandsworth) | Mitcham – Phipps |
| | East Molesey | Wickford (2) |
| | Ewell | Tollsworth (Chaldon) |
| | Hartington (Kingston) | Wallington (fulling) |
| | Kingswood (Ewell) | West Molesey (2) |
| | Merton | |
| | Pachensham (Leatherhead) | |
| | Polesden Lacey | |
| | Shelwood (Ewell) | |
| | South Tadworth (Banstead) | |
| | Tollsworth (Chaldon) | |
| | Tooting Bec (1394-1422) | |
| | Wimbledon (1363-76) | |
| Sussex | | Duncton |
| | | Perching (windmill) |
| | | Poynings |
| | | Preston |
| Wiltshire | Great Chelworth (Cricklade) | |
| Yorkshire | Akenberg | |
| | Belagh | |

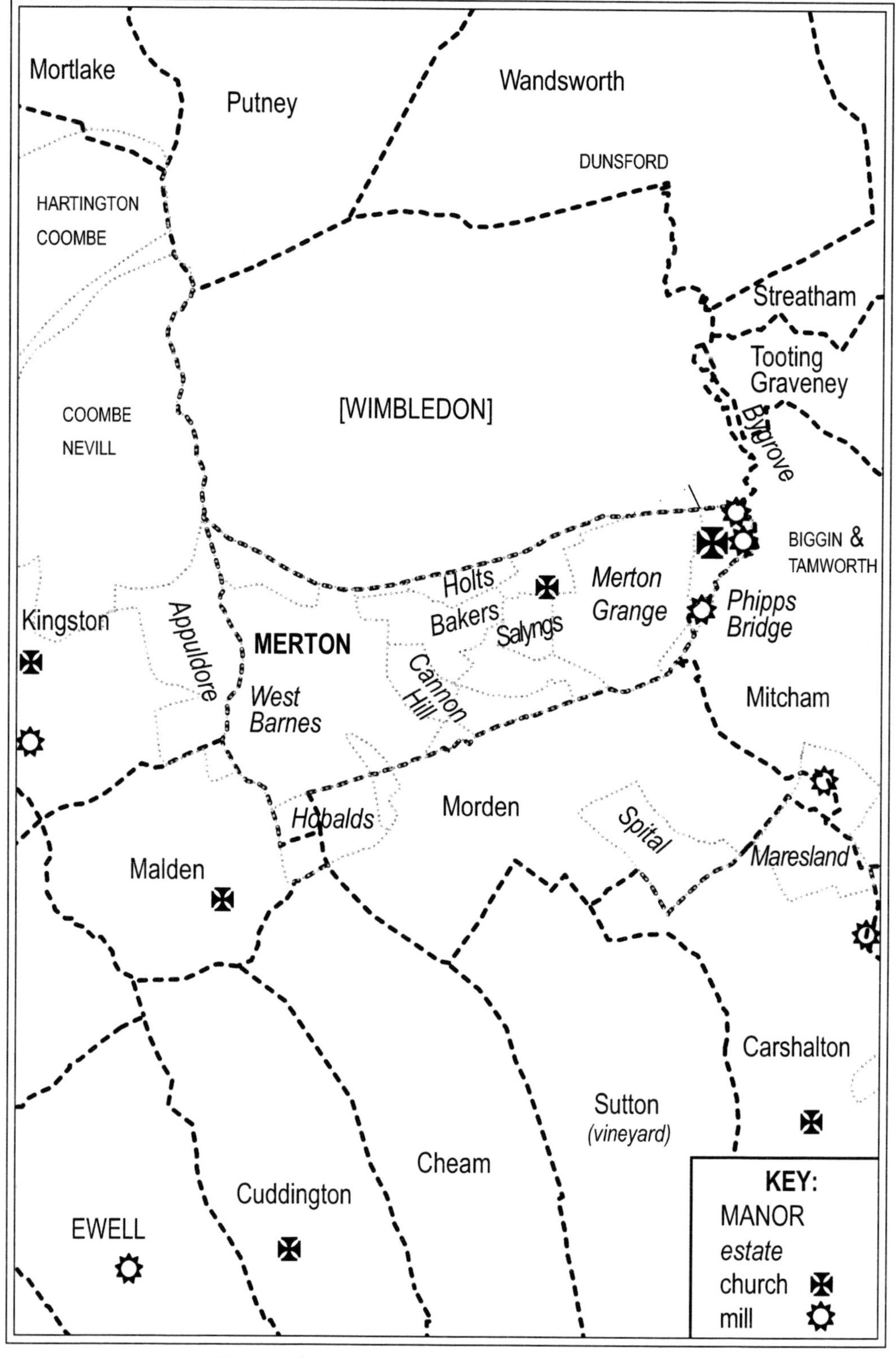


*Properties belonging to Merton priory in and around Merton*

## 15. A Local Landlord

by Peter Hopkins

*"Honest labour bears a lovely face;*
*Then hey nonny, nonny, hey nonny, nonny."*
Thomas Dekker *Patient Grissil*

After Henry I granted permission in 1121 for the ville of Merton to be given to the priory, "Gilbert ... returned to Merton, and on the following day he summoned to church the men of the town and gave them into the power of the prior".[247]

The villagers were not merely the prior's tenants, they were "in his power". As the prior's villeins they owed him a cash rent for the land and dwelling they held from him; they had to attend his courts and submit to his justice (he was entitled to set up a gallows in Merton);[248] they had to pay him fines for a range of activities – for permission to live outside the manor, for daughters to marry, for sons to take holy orders, for licence to sell their own corn or to cut their own timber, and at death to give him their best beast as heriot as well as an entry fine payable by the heir; they owed payments in kind, such as eggs at Easter; and every week they were required to work one day on his land and even more at harvest time.

By the 14th century it would appear that some of these demands had been relaxed, no doubt in exchange for further cash payment, but with the labour shortage caused by the Black Death the priory decided to reinstate the labour services and other requirements. This met with fierce opposition from the tenantry:-

In 1348, "litigation arose concerning the customs of the manor of Merton. Stephen in the Hale, John Jakes, Richard Est and other men of the Prior of Merton complained of his unscrupulous exaction of services and customs such as had not been wont when the king held this demesne. The men alleged they held only by fealty and rent; but the prior exacted one day's forced labour a week, and compelled their services for mending a ditch called Le Brok, shearing the prior's sheep for two days (for which they only received ½d. a day), mowing his meadows for a day and a half, with pay of 1½d. a day, each man also having to find three men for three days to carry the prior's hay, and for three half-days to take the grain, for nothing. Further, the prior exacted for twelve days a year twenty-four men to reap his corn with an allowance of ¾d. for four days' food, and ½d. for eight days' food. Further, they had to sift the prior's malt from the feast of St. Andrew [30th Nov.] to Christmas, with a 4d. fine for any leakage, and to harrow 1 acre for a loaf worth ¼d.; besides which the prior exacted ten eggs a year from each on Good Friday. The upkeep of the bridge between Merton and Kingston was also one of their tasks. Their sons could not escape this bondage by taking holy orders without paying the prior a fine, and none might sell their own corn or cut down their own timber without the prior's licence. To all these and other allegations the prior could only aver the men were his serfs, a charge they denied, and to prevent them from prosecuting the suit he tried to impoverish them by heavily distraining them by their goods and chattels."[249]

Relations between the prior and his tenants were not always good. An undated petition to a king from his 'poor tenants of ancient demesne of manor of Merton' complains of extreme measures taken by the prior. He and a fellow canon, William de Kent (Cantia), were accused of entering the tenants' houses, breaking open their chests and violently taking away their proofs of title to their properties. The tenants appealed to the king that the prior should be made to answer for such abuse of their heritage, 'of which their predecessors had been enfeoffed by King Harold, and that the king would grant protection to his poor tenants of Merton'.[250]

The parish church was also in the priory's possession. As rector of the church it enjoyed the right to receive tithes of their tenants' crops and livestock, and also to receive mortuary payments and other oblations. Unlike other rectories appropriated to the priory, Merton did not have a vicar, as the church was served by the canons, and later by chaplains appointed by the priory.[251]

By the end of the 15th century few of the customary tenants held land in the open fields of the manor, most having just a small croft adjoining their dwelling. Several tenants held more than one copyhold tenement, and these were often merged into a single property. The proximity of the priory attracted a succession of wealthy citizens of London. In 1487 Thomas Lok headed a consortium of London mercers in buying the freehold property opposite the parish church, later known as Church House. This property stayed in the Lock family until 1646. Thomas also bought several copyhold properties in Merton, but sold them all in 1498 to another citizen of London, a clothseller named Lawrence Aylemer, who in turn sold them in 1500. The properties included two tenements, two messuages, five cottages, and numerous tofts, crofts, parcels of enclosed land, and strips in the open arable fields and meadows.[252]

Within the next few years the priory took possession of all but three acres (1.2 ha) of the arable land formerly held by its customary tenants, and created large compact farms. This was achieved partly through land defaulting to the priory on the death of tenants without heirs, partly by repossession of land where the tenant had broken the 'customs of the manor' by letting his dwelling fall into ruin or by cutting timber without permission, and partly by the 'voluntary' surrender of the property by the tenant.[252]

When the priory was dissolved in 1538 there was one freehold tenement in Merton, and 13 copyholds, as well as two tenements, six cottages and three parcels of land held 'at will' or leased on a yearly basis.[253] The large compact farms were also leased to tenants for fixed terms – West Barnes (579 acres – 235 ha); Merton Grange (396 acres – 160 ha); Merton Holts (180 acres – 73 ha), and Salyngs (no acreage given). Even the rectorial right to receive tithes was leased, together with "a tenement and parcel of land on the west side of the parish church, with a barn and close called the parsonage barn". 'Canondownehill' (60 acres – 24 ha), several parcels of land between Kingston Road and Cannon Hill Lane which later became Bakers Farm (146 acres – 59 ha), and various parcels of meadow and pasture in Merton, Morden and Mitcham (144 acres – 58 ha), remained in hand as demesne land, along with the precinct itself.[254]

A further 30 acres in Merton formed part of another priory estate called Hobalds, mainly in Morden (82½ acres – 33 ha), but with a further 30 acres adjoining in Malden. North-east Surrey Crematorium and its cemetery now occupy most of the site of the farm in Lower Morden. The estate was given to the priory in the early 13th century.[255] Another estate in Morden, 'le Spital', between Central Road and Farm Road, had also come into the priory's possession by the end of the 13th century.[256]

The priory also held several estates in neighbouring Mitcham, most of them since the 13th century. By 1538 these included "the Manor of Byggyng and Tamworth, certain land called Amery landes in Micham, and land called Mareshlandes in Micham and Carshalton".[257] It also held land called "Bygrave Hyll in Mycham", leased with lands known as "Hydefeld and Balam mede in Clapham".[258] It also received rents from certain lands at "Pyppisbrigg and in Bygrove Hyll and elsewhere in Totyng Graveney".[259]

To the west of Merton the priory held land called "Appuldore in Maldon and Kyngestone", which later formed part of Blagdon Farm.[258] Further Appuldore lands were attached to its manor of "Combnevell",[260] which it had received in 1423/4.[261] Also in Coombe was the Manor of "Chartington" or Hartington Coombe, held since at least the beginning of the 13th century.[262] Other possessions in the Kingston district included the manor of Berwell,[263] and "the manor of Chessyngdon at le Hoke in Chessington".[258] It also held "the Rectory of Kyngeston, with appurtenances in Kyngeston, Surveton, Norveton, Hampp, Hathe, Petrysham, Cayho and Shene."[264] The priory had also held the advowson of Malden church from the late 12th century until it was given to Walter de Merton in 1265, towards the endowment of Merton College, Oxford.

In nearby Wandsworth Merton priory held the Manor of Dunsford, since the mid 12th century at least, and a "tenement in Wannesworth called le Garrett".[265]

Just down the A24, or rather Stane Street, was the manor of Ewell which included Kingswood. This was a 'gift' of King Henry II in 1155/6.[266] Also attached to this manor in 1538 was "certain land called Holbroke in Okeley".[267] The manor of Shelwood, including "lands in Lye, Horley, Charlwood and Newdegate", had historically been part of their manor of Ewell.[268] The priory also held 118 acres (48 ha) of land in Cuddington.[269]

Other Surrey manors included Tollsworth in Chaldon,[270] Little Ashtead,[271] Cannon Court in Fetcham,[272] Polesden Lacey,[273] and South Tadworth in Banstead.[273] The priory had held a manor in Molesey until 1535 when Henry VIII exchanged it for property in Staffordshire.[274] All these manors had been in the priory's possession since the 12th or early 13th century. The priory also briefly held the leases of three other Surrey manors

– the Archbishop of Canterbury's manor of Wimbledon for 13 years from 1363/4;[275] the royal manor of Banstead from 1377;[276] and the manor of Tooting Bec from around 1394 to 1422.[277] In all these manors it exercised full manorial jurisdiction, as it did in the manor of Merton itself.

Also in Surrey, Merton priory held full rectorial rights in Carshalton, Effingham and Cuddington,[278] though part of the tithe went to support the vicar. It appointed the rectors of Ewhurst, Guildford, and Long Ditton and received pensions from them, having held the advowson of each of these churches since the 12th century. It was also entitled to portions of tithes from "the farm of Tullesworth in Chaldon and from mills in Carshalton".[279]

Mills, both for grinding corn and for fulling cloth, often appear in the priory's records. As well as the Carshalton mills it held interests in mills in Ewell, Fetcham, Kingston, Mitcham, Molesey, and Tandridge, as well as, of course, in Merton itself.

The priory also had a quarry at Tollsworth,[280] a vineyard at Sutton,[281] and a fishery on the Thames, with weirs at Kew and Brentford.[282]

It also received rents from properties in Beddington, Carshalton, Chaldon, Chelsham, Chessington, Crowhurst, Ditton, East Horsley, Fetcham, Hook, Horley, Horne, Kingston, Leatherhead, Malden, Mickleham, Polesden, Sutton, Tandridge, Tolworth, Wallington, Walton on Thames and Warlingham,[283] as well as from various properties in London and Southwark.[284]

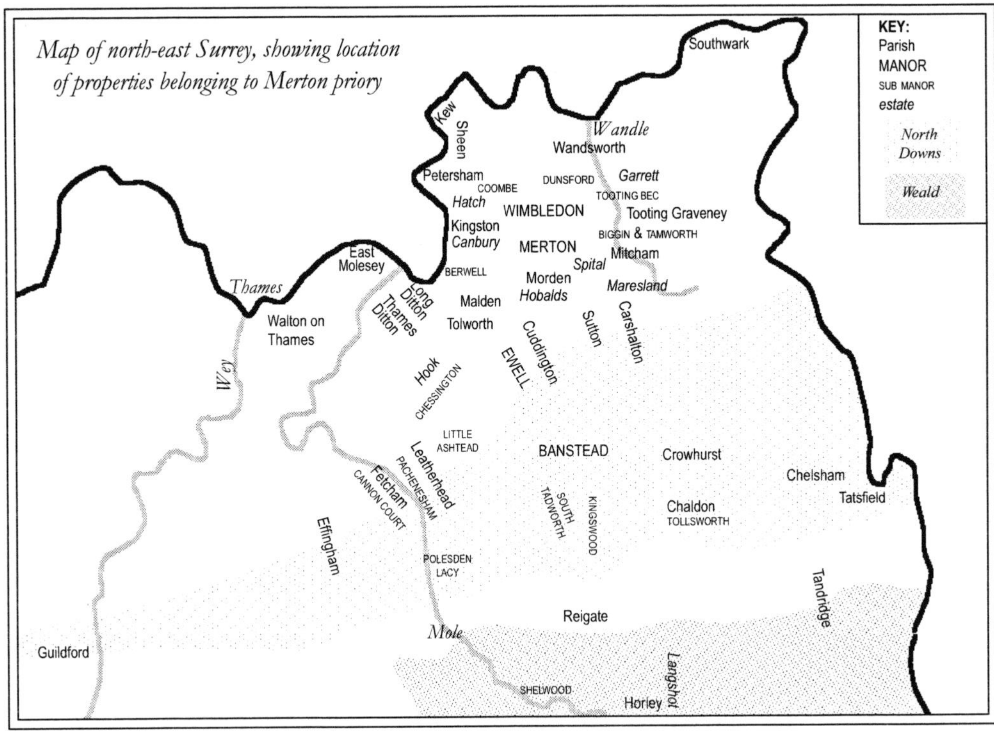

Map of north-east Surrey, showing location of properties belonging to Merton priory

# 16. A Glimpse of Greatness

*"Be not afraid of greatness … Some have greatness thrust upon them."*
*Twelfth Night* Act 2

*Consecration of Becket as archbishop, based on British Library Royal MS.2.B.7*

## Becket

The priory's associations with Thomas Becket were not restricted to his education (see Chapter 6 – Centre of Learning). He was instrumental in obtaining benefactions to complete the building of the priory. On being elected to the archbishopric at Westminster abbey on 23 May 1162, his priority was to ride straight to Merton with a large following of clerics and lay folk. Here he adopted the habit of an Augustinian canon and chose brother Robert to be his confessor.[285]

*Assassination of Becket, from an ancient painting on a board hung at the head of the tomb of Henry IV in Canterbury cathedral*

Robert had probably been a student with him some 35 years earlier and stayed with Thomas until his dying day at the martyrdom in Canterbury cathedral.

## Hubert Walter

When Richard I came to the throne in 1189, Hubert Walter was made bishop of Salisbury. He had already taken a vow to join the crusades, and he left England on 16 September 1190 and was present at the siege of Acre on 12 October. When justiciar Ranulf de Glanville's death was followed by that of archbishop Baldwin on 19 November, Hubert had greatness thrust upon him and became the chief spiritual leader. The historian Ralph de Diceto refers to him as "the bishop of Salisbury and the English".[286] On his return to England he was consecrated archbishop of Canterbury on 20 April 1193, and "he considered it advisable to become a monk and was received as an Austin (Augustinian) canon at Merton".[287]

## The Interdict

King John had a poor relationship with the pope and the barons. The country was laid under interdict by Innocent III on 23 March 1208 and subsequently the king was excommunicated. For six years the churches in England were officially closed and silent. Stephen Langton, the pope's choice for the new archbishop of Canterbury, spent five years (1208-13) at Pontigny, France, awaiting permission from king John to proceed to Canterbury. Services at Merton priory would have continued as normal, for the bishops of Norwich and Winchester refused to act on the interdict. The abbots of the London monasteries were not so fortunate, as the king kept them prisoner until they had paid sufficient money for their release. Many of the bishops, relieved of their duties, fled to the continent and John seized their revenues.

John despatched five special messengers to negotiate with the pope and promised to abide by their deliberations. On 27 February 1213 the pope declared that as only three of the messengers had presented themselves, nothing could be agreed. One of the missing messengers was Richard of Merton. Finally the king accepted the pope's choice on 15 May 1213 and ceded the kingdom to the pope. Langton arrived in England and went to Merton priory on 1 August 1213 where he met with the bishops of Ely, Lincoln and London.[288] This meeting resolved the problems of the interdict, which was lifted in June 1214.

## Runnymede

The king still had problems with the rebel barons who took control of London on 17 May 1215. John found himself restricted mainly south of the River Thames, with the court based at Windsor. On 5 June he made a royal progress from Windsor to Winchester and returned by way of Merton where he stayed for three days. From Merton on 8 June, he issued letters of safe conduct for a baronial deputation to make peace.[289] This was the start of the negotiations which led to the meeting at Runnymede. The pope was angry that John had agreed to such a document and the king of France decided to send the dauphin Louis to claim the throne of England. He landed at Sandwich on 2 June 1216, captured Rochester on 6 June and entered London. Most of the barons supported Louis who also captured Reigate and Guildford. In October king John died and young Henry III, aged nine, became king of England.

## Peace Conference

The invader from France was unable to advance far from London and reinforcements were denied to the dauphin by the action of Hubert de Burgh off Dover in August 1217. A peace conference was called by the pope's legate, Gualo, which took place on an island near Kingston. Merton provided accommodation for Gualo from 17 to 23 September. Following the conference, Louis the dauphin, the queen mother, the young king and nobles of England and France came to Merton. The dauphin was offered generous terms with an indemnity of 10,000 marks (£6,666) to finance his withdrawal from England. Louis was escorted from Merton to Dover on 22 September 1217.[289]

## Council of Merton

Parliament met at Merton in 1236 to pass some of the country's most important medieval laws. The bishops and barons stayed at Merton from 20 to 27 January.

Henry III had married Eleanor, daughter of the count of Provence, and the barons feared that the king would rely on foreign advisors and disregard the traditional counsel with the barons. He had already invited Bretons and Provençals to occupy royal castles and posts in his court.

Magna Carta had formulated fundamental freedoms for all subjects, but written parliamentary law had to wait for the Statute of Merton. It consists of 11 chapters dealing with the rights of widows, the enclosure of commons and waste lands provided that sufficient land was left available to satisfy customary tenants' rights, and bastardy. It was the last item which brought forth the famous words

*Two columns from the Statute of Merton 1236 (reproduced by permission of the British Library Cott Claud DII fo.145-145v)*

*nolumus leges Angliae mutare* – "we are unwilling to change the laws of England". The laws passed remained in part on the statute book of Parliament for over 700 years. This was the first declaration on points of law i.e. the first statute and consequently the first entry in the Statute Book. One of the witnesses to the statute was Simon de Montfort.

## Walter de Merton

Walter de Merton is said to have "moulded the whole history of Oxford and Cambridge Universities".[290] He was probably born in Basingstoke about 1210 and educated at Merton priory. His studies continued at Oxford under Adam de Marisco and he was accepted into minor orders but never became a canon regular.

From 1231 he assisted the prior of Merton in a legal capacity, was appointed by the prior parson of Cuddington in 1235, and to be his attorney at the Hampshire Eyre in January/February 1236.[291] By 1238 his parents had died and Walter adopted the name of de Merton.

By 1240, as a chancery clerk, he had earned enough in fees to obtain the encumbered manors of Malden with Chessington and Farleigh in Surrey from the crown which had custody of them during the minority of Richard de Clare from 1230 until he came of age in 1240.

From 1249 Walter was appointed a king's clerk and while Henry III was in France with the chancellor 1259/60, Walter held the royal seal and set up the chancery at

*Walter de Merton's tomb in Rochester cathedral (photograph by the author)*

Malden where he sent out the king's orders acting as chancellor. He became chancellor in 1261 and was granted 400 marks (£266.66) per annum.

De Merton had been considering the education of eight of his nephews and no doubt conferred with the prior of Merton regarding possibilities. In 1261 Walter obtained a charter from Richard de Clare, now overlord of the manors of Malden and Farleigh, and they were conveyed to Merton priory. Late in 1263 the manors were allotted to support the education of Walter's nephews. The management of the college was at Malden from 1262, probably because of its nearness to Merton priory, less than five miles away. The king was often governing from Merton and Walter could be in touch with affairs of state as well as his educational scheme. On 7 January 1264 he set down the charter for his new college.

Meanwhile in July 1263, Simon de Montfort recovered his position of power and dismissed de Merton as chancellor, after Malden had been attacked by robbers on 13 June and occupied for three days.

In setting up his educational establishment, Walter de Merton borrowed from his experiences at the priory, with the idea of a corporate life under a common rule and head, and supported by secure endowments. But he expressly prohibited scholars from taking vows, and any who did should forfeit his scholarship.

The foundation was self-governing and not under the control of any outside body such as a religious house. It controlled its academic standards and opened the way for secular as well as religious learning. The final statutes were issued in August 1274 when the warden, bailiffs and ministers were transferred from Malden to the permanent home at Oxford.

When Peterhouse was founded at Cambridge, the licence stated that the scholars "shall live together according to the rule of the scholars at Oxford who are called of Merton". Thus Walter de Merton moulded both Oxford and Cambridge Universities.

The founder was made bishop of Rochester and consecrated by archbishop Kilwardby on 21 October 1274.

### Royal Councils

In January 1255 king Henry III called for a council meeting at Merton to discuss how to meet his expenses abroad. It was agreed that the king should tallage (tax) his demesne land throughout England, which meant crown lands. London's charters excluded Londoners from paying tallage and they refused to pay. The mayor was summoned to Merton and the king demanded 3000 marks (£2,000). The Londoners went away and returned saying that they were willing to grant 2000 marks (£1333) as an aid, but would not pay more.[292]

*Edward I presiding over the House of Lords.*
*Based on a drawing made in the 15th or 16th century, now in the Royal Library Windsor.*
*Note the bishops and mitred abbots on the left and in the foreground.*

Modern parliament began with the council summoned by Simon de Montfort on behalf of the captive king. The prior of Merton was called to attend on the 20 January 1265 by a writ dated at Woodstock 24 December 1264.[293] He was summoned again in 1300.[294] The prior attended royal councils as a 'mitred abbot' and sat as a spiritual lord until 1327 (see Chapter 13 – Royal Visitors Jan.1327).

## Consecrations

Whilst consecrations of a bishop could take place at Merton, the enthronement could only be at the cathedral of his diocese which contained his seat of teaching and governing. The Latin for chair is *sedes* from which is derived the bishop's 'see', and *kathedra* is Greek for seat, hence 'cathedral'.

In 1131 Robert of Bethune, prior of Llanthony, was at Merton where he was impressed by the standards here.[295] Whilst at Merton he was consecrated bishop of Hereford.

Elias of Radnor or Helyas, treasurer of Hereford, was consecrated bishop of Llandaff at Merton in December 1230. The monks of Canterbury complained that the ceremony should have taken place there.[296]

On 26 February 1273 Robert Kilwardby was consecrated archbishop of Canterbury at Merton priory, following difficulties between the pope, king and the Canterbury monks.[297] In 1274 he crowned Edward I and queen Eleanor, at Westminster. On 7 April 1275 he returned to Merton in order to consecrate Robert Burnell as bishop of Bath and Wells.[298] In 1276 Kilwardby chose to stay at Merton's grange at Upton, Buckinghamshire.[299]

## Convocations

Church convocations were held at Merton in 1258 and 1306.[300] These were church councils, and the archbishops could summon a Provincial council without referring to the king except if it involved raising taxation. Clerical assemblies were not encouraged by Henry III as they usually only met when there were taxes to be resisted. He termed the gathering of 1258 an illegitimate *convocatio* (calling together) and subsequent church councils were known as convocations.

On 19 April 1258 archbishop Boniface, at the pleading of the pope's envoy, summoned a convocation to meet at Merton on Thursday 6 June. The pope's envoy felt confident that he could influence the clergy to support the pope and the king. Summoned to the meeting at Merton were the heads of the great monasteries and all archdeacons. The preamble stated that it was to consider papal demands, including the tallage of three marks (£2) to be levied on every monastery in England, and to provide for the restoration of ecclesiastical liberty. To the horror of the envoy, who was present at Merton, archbishop Boniface made a vigorous denunciation of lay encroachments of clerical rights by both pope and king. The meeting put on record the grievances expressed by Grosseteste, bishop of Lincoln, who had died in 1253, and resolved that the dire oppression of the church must be remedied. Subsequently Henry III asked the pope to abrogate the resolutions, which he did.[301]

In 1306 archbishop Winchelsea presided over a convocation of the clergy of the Province at Merton and laid down the statutory period for feudal tenants to pay tithes to their parish priests. This was from shearing time until Martinmas (11 November). The convocation also set out the items that parishioners had to provide; "missal, chalice, vestments, crosses, incense, thurible, lights and bells … ".[302]

## Knights Templar

This was an international and military Order arising out of the crusades. The Templars amassed great wealth and became international bankers. Henry II gave the Templars sufficient money to pay for 200 knights for a year in the Holy Land, in expiation for Becket's murder.

At the beginning of the 14th century in France, king Philippe IV found them arrogant and unruly but rich. He tried to join the Order as a postulant but was rejected. In 1303 and 1304 two popes mysteriously died (Boniface VIII and Benedict XI). King Philippe then secured the election of his own candidate, the archbishop of Bordeaux, to the papacy. He became Clement V in 1305.

In both London and Paris there were murmurs in 1306 about the Templars' vices and infidelity. King Philippe issued sealed and secret orders to his seneschals throughout France which were to be opened simultaneously and implemented at dawn on Friday 13 October 1307. All Templars in France were seized and placed under arrest by the king's men and their goods confiscated. In Paris and other parts of France, knights were burned at the stake.

On 20 December 1307 the sheriffs of England were instructed by Letters Close to arrest all members of the Order "on the Wednesday next after Epiphany in the morning" (8 January 1308), and to take inventories of their possessions.[303] In September 1308 Walter de Geddinges, sheriff of Surrey, held an inquisition at Guildford before John de Foxele.[304] Templars were sent to the castles of London, Lincoln, York and Dublin.

*Two Templars on a single horse, based on a drawing by Matthew Paris in his* Chronica majora. *Corpus Christi College, Cambridge, MS 26:110v.*

In England and Wales in 1308, there were 165 Templars consisting of 6 knights, 41 chaplains and 118 sergeants. Their gross annual revenue was £4,720. In Surrey they owned the manors of Caterham, Merrow (1/3rd), Temple Elfold and Wychyflet in Southwark.[305]

Papal judicial enquiries began in London on Monday 20 October 1309 but elicited nothing derogatory. The master of the Templars refused to admit to any crimes and was kept in the Tower "confined with double irons". He did not long survive this treatment.[306]

Six English Templars were convicted in July 1311, all given light sentences and sent to monasteries as a penance. One of them, Stephen de Stapelbrigg, when examined on 23 June 1311, had admitted that he had been made to spit on his hand near the cross and to deny the Saviour and the Virgin.[306] He was delivered to Merton priory to do penance in 1312 whilst the king ordered Henry de Cobham, keeper of the Templars' lands in Surrey to provide a maintenance allowance of fourpence (2p) per day.[307]

Later, de Stapelbrigg escaped from Merton and was re-arrested at Salisbury. He was sent to London where he was examined in 1319 and finally sent to Christchurch priory, Hampshire (now in Dorset) to do penance. Thomas Totty (or Stotty) was another Templar sent to end his days at Merton, in the 1320s.[308]

In 1311 pope Clement V held a church council in Vienne, south of Lyon. On 8 September the prior of Merton wrote to him stating that three canons from Thornton, Cirencester and Waltham would be his proctors at the council.[309] This met on 16 December and demanded the suppression of the Order of Knights Templar. The Order was officially dissolved by a Bull published 15 August 1312 and its possessions confiscated. The papal Bull was never proclaimed in Scotland and many French Templars made their way there and fought for Scotland in 1314, helping to defeat the English at Bannockburn.

After Edward II had taken his pick of properties, he transferred the Templars' possessions by a statute in 1323 to the Knights Hospitaller of St John.

*Knights Templar,*
*based on contemporary depictions*

## The English Church in the 14th Century

Nothing did more to undermine the prestige of the papacy in England than the 70 years residence of the papacy at Avignon 1309-1378. The popes were Frenchmen and tools of the French kings. (See above: 'Knights Templar'). Into Oxford in 1370 came a tutor named John Wycliffe who spoke against involvement of the senior clergy in the affairs of state. He also expounded anti-papal views and was supported by the king in resisting the claims of the papacy regarding tribute granted originally by king John in acknowledgement of the fealty of the kingdom. Gregory XI issued bulls including one to the university of Oxford to examine Wycliffe's 'erroneous' doctrines. In 1378 Wycliffe began to translate the scriptures into English for ordinary people and sent out 'poor preachers' to visit the villages with pamphlets and parts of scripture. The middle class heard him gladly but many were afraid of his views on transubstantiation.[310] Wycliffe was called to a convocation at Lambeth in 1378 but was supported by John of Gaunt who advocated reforms against clerical abuses. He was also supported by social reformers who played their part in the peasant rising of 1381. A further convocation was held on 18 November 1382 at Oxford when 24 statements of doctrine were condemned and Wycliffe banished from the city.

## Michael Kympton

Into this situation came a canon of Merton under prior Robert de Windsor (1368-1403). Michael Kympton no doubt came from Kimpton, Hertfordshire, whose church had been appropriated by Merton Priory. He was ordained priest in 1369, and in 1395 attended the provincial chapter of the Augustinian Order at Northampton in place of the prior (see Chapter 9). In 1397 he was appointed a professor of divinity at Oxford[311] and in 1399 Richard II issued a brief to certain prelates "including Master Michael, canon of Merton ... to appear in their proper person before him at Oxford ... to declare their counsel and advice concerning certain nefarious matters of schism in the Church of God".[312]

Wycliffe had died on 31 December 1384 but there were still many followers of his teachings. In 1428, 44 years after his death, pope Martin V ordered his bones to be dug up and destroyed.

On 30 June 1403 Michael Kympton was made prior of Merton[313] and in October 1403 he set up the keeping of the manorial records of Tooting, the manor which the priory had leased from the abbey of Bec since 13 December 1394 (see MHS *Bulletin* 151, Sept. 2004, p.12). In 1408 he ordered the compilation of a survey of the manor of Ewell, the Register or Memorial of Ewell. He died in 1413. During an archaeological excavation at the chapter house site in the 1980s part of a grave inscription plate was discovered bearing the possible name of KYMPTON.

## Thomas Paynell

Paynell (d.1564) was a brilliant translator of Latin into English, and spent most of his life at Merton priory until the Dissolution. He was educated at Merton and went on to St Mary's College (now defunct), Oxford, which had been set up by the Augustinian Order to foster sons of those houses. He returned to Merton priory in 1528 to take up literary and medical studies, and became an acolyte. He was also a member of Gray's Inn, London. Between 1530 and 1538 he published many books and, being a disciple of Erasmus, once an Augustinian canon, he translated his *De Contemptu Mundi* in 1533. He dedicated it to Mary, dowager-queen of France by "your daily orator". In 1537 he published Erasmus's *The Comparation of a Vyrgyn and a Martyr.* This was dedicated to John Ramsey, prior of Merton, at whose request Paynell had undertaken the translation. He wrote over 30 books and was often on royal service as a diplomat following the Dissolution. He became chaplain to Henry VIII.[314] On his death in 1564, Paynell bequeathed 110 books and five manuscripts to St John's College, Oxford.

## Richard Benese

Benese was at Oxford from 1514 to 1519 and became a clerk in priests' orders about 1527 before becoming a canon of Merton. In 1530 he was succentor, assisting in leading the singing in choir. He saw the need for better measurement of land and no doubt improved the recording of the estates belonging to the priory. He measured irregularly shaped fields/woods by using standard geometric shapes – squares, rectangles and triangles. He valued land arbitrarily by size and use. An acre (0.4 ha) was worth a mark (£0.66), a rood – 5 shillings (£0.25). Three days' work was a shilling (£0.05), one day's a groat (£0.02).

In 1537 he produced his book on surveying "newly invented and compiled by Sir Rychard Benese, Chanon [sic] of Merton Abbey".[315] The preface was written by a fellow brother and writer, Thomas Paynell (see above) and further editions were published long after his death. In 1538 he was one of the signatories of the deed of surrender of the priory and was granted a pension of £6 13s 4d (£6.66) p.a. Benese had been made Surveyor of the King's Household based at Hampton Court and checked all estimates of men and materials for the building work at Hampton Court, Oatlands and Nonsuch. Like Thomas Paynell he became a royal chaplain.

Benese held many offices, including precentor of Hereford, prebendary of Lincoln, rector of Beddington Portion and Long Ditton, Surrey, and All Hallows, Honey Lane, London. He died in January 1547 and was buried at Long Ditton.

## Important Visitors

The legate Pandolph who negotiated with king John in1211 over his excommunication was elected bishop of Norwich in 1216, following the death of John de Gray who ignored the interdict. Pandolph stayed at Merton on 3 April 1220.[316]

Boniface of Savoy was elected archbishop of Canterbury in 1241 but did not come to England until 1243. So on 2 June he came straight to Merton "to examine and confirm or reject" Robert Passelewe as bishop of Chichester, and certain other bishops-elect. The record concludes that about 9 o'clock there was such a severe tempest, as had not been seen at Merton for many years before.[317] The new archbishop rejected Passelewe as bishop, and the pope agreed. Boniface returned to Merton in 1258 to preside over the convocation referred to above (see Convocations).

For the year long stay of Edmund Rich in 1213, the sanctuary for Hubert de Burgh in 1232, the visit of archbishop Peckham, and the month's stay of William of Wykeham in 1376, see Chapter 12 – Hospitality.

Throughout the centuries many important visitors died at the priory. These include:

Ewan, bishop of Evreux, Normandy, in 1139 (see Chapter 12 – Hospitality).

Richmond, abbot of Bruern, Oxfordshire, in February 1176.[318]

John, abbot of Waverley, Surrey, on 16 September 1201.[319]

Henry, prince of England, on 14 October 1274 (see Chapter 13 – Royal Visitors).

John Peckham, archbishop of Canterbury, on 8 December 1292 (see Chapter 12 – Hospitality).

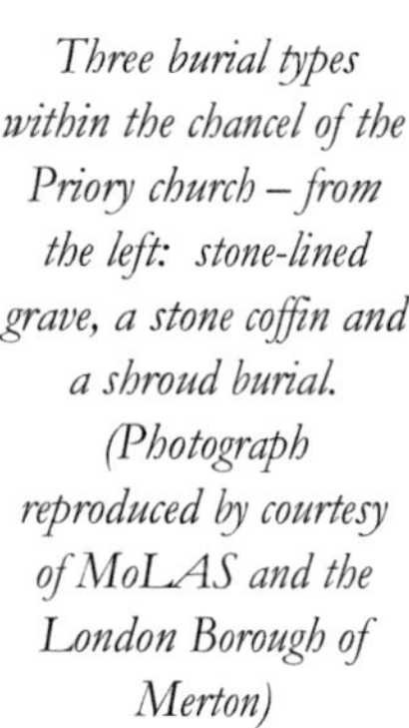

*Three burial types within the chancel of the Priory church – from the left: stone-lined grave, a stone coffin and a shroud burial. (Photograph reproduced by courtesy of MoLAS and the London Borough of Merton)*

# 17. Pastures New

*"At last he rose, and twitched his mantle blue:*
*Tomorrow to fresh woods, and pastures new."*
John Milton *Lycidas*

When a novice 'professed' to his calling and took the monastic vows of poverty, chastity and obedience, other conditions were imposed. One was *stabilitas* i.e. to swear to spend his life in the monastery of his profession.

Sometimes circumstances forced or enabled canons to change houses, and in fact *transitus*, the transfer, was practised throughout monastic times. Canon law allowed for this, but a member had to seek permission from his superior, and any move from one Order to another had to be to a stricter and more austere house. A regular canon could become a Cistercian monk but any move in the opposite direction was not permitted. However if an Augustinian canon left to become a Premonstratensian canon with its stricter and harsher life, he was likely to find the verminous clothing became an irritant to the flesh.[320] The term 'strictness' gave rise to debates between canons and monks as there was no accepted measure of strictness. The Observances of Barnwell priory pointed out that there were many different paths to the celestial Jerusalem, some of which were stricter and some less strict.[321] Anselm of Laon (d.1117) formulated the phrase *diversi sed non adversi* (diverse but not contrary) to describe the importance of all the various Orders. A few of the first canons at Merton may have transferred from Aldgate Priory.[97]

After 20 years as prior of Merton, Walter left Merton in 1218 to go to Grande Chartreuse near Grenoble, France "despising the riches and pomp of the world and longing for the quiet of solitude".[322] Walter had entertained king John in 1204 and 1215, the dauphin of France in 1217 and the nobility of England. At Grande Chartreuse, the Carthusians lived the lives of virtual hermits, each in his own lodging. They lived alone in perpetual silence save on Sundays and festivals.

William de Cantia, in 1258, tried to reform Merton priory and its arrangements, but was banished to another, unknown, Augustinian house.[146]

In 1304 the bishop granted letters dimissory (permission to be ordained elsewhere) in respect of four brethren.[323] One was Ralph de Waltham, who subsequently returned to Merton as a canon when acting as one of the proctors at the election of prior Thomas de Kent on 25 April 1335.[324] Further dimissory letters were granted in 1398 and 1401.[325] In the 15th century it would appear that it became necessary to obtain not only the bishop's permission, but papal authority as well. Clement Saunderson is referred to as a canon of Merton in 1485 and 1492.[326] His brother John Saunderson of Streatham died in 1490 and left his estate to Clement[327] who applied to the pope for dispensation to become a parish priest. He was informed about 1494 that "although professed in the Augustinian Order he could receive any benefice with or without cure … even if a parish church or its perpetual vicarage was usually assigned to secular clerics".[328]

In 1387 John Cherteseye, a canon at Newstead, Nottinghamshire, was transferred to Merton "to be safely kept there, and there to be dealt with as the rule prescribe". He had been the cause of scandal at Newstead, "from various excesses and faults".[150]

The extent of movement throughout the period can be gauged from a list.

| Name | Former house | New position | Date left | Date of death | Source |
|---|---|---|---|---|---|
| Guy | canon of Merton | prior of Taunton | 1120 | May 1124 | Colker (69) p.254 |
| | | prior of Bodmin | 1123 | | |
| Guy | canon of Merton | prior of Southwick | c1185 | 3 Nov. 1206 | Heads I p.184 |
| Martin | canon of Merton | prior of Southwark | c1205 | 11 June 1218 | Heads I p.184<br>Heads II p.460 |
| Richard de Morins (Mores) | deacon of Merton | prior of Dunstable | 21 Sept. 1202 | 9 April 1242 | Heales p.58<br>Heads I p.163 |
| Henry de Mareis | canon of Merton | prior of Carlisle | 25 Aug. 1214 | ?1217 | Heales p.70<br>Heads I p.158<br>Heads II p.359 |
| Walter | prior of Merton (1198-1218) | monk at Chartreuse | Sept. 1218 | | Heales p.75<br>Heads II p.421 |
| Giles de Bourne | prior of Merton (1222-1231) | monk at Beaulieu | 23 Jan. 1231 | Sept. 1231 | Heads II p.422<br>SRS 32(1983)p.475 |
| William de Campesete | canon of Merton | prior of Bilsington | 1253 | Oct.1255 | Heales p.137<br>Heads II p.336 |
| Walter of Rye | canon of Merton | prior of Bilsington | 1255 | Oct 1261 | Heales p.137<br>Heads II p.336 |
| William de Cantia | canon of Merton | | 3rd June 1258 | | Heales pp.133, 299 |
| Ralph of South Malling | canon of Merton | prior of Bilsington | Oct. 1261 | Nov.1272/3 | Heales p.138<br>Heads II p.336 |
| John Cherteseye | canon of Newstead | canon of Merton | 25 Oct. 1387 | | Heales p.274 |
| John de Yakesley | canon of Merton | prior of Reigate | 1395 (election annulled by pope but authority given) | | Heales p.288 |
| Thomas Wandsworth (alias Munday) | canon of Merton | prior of Bodmin | April 1534 | c1549 | see Chapter 18 |

Heads I = *Heads of Religious Houses I, 940-1216* – Knowles, Brooke & London (eds) CUP 1972
Heads II = *Heads of Religious Houses II, 1216-1377* – Smith & London (eds) CUP 2001
SRS 32 (1983) = *The 1235 Surrey Eyre* Vol.2 – Surrey Record Society XXXII 1983

# Elections of last priors and remaining canons

| Born | Name | 1485 | 1492 | 1502 | 1520 | 1530 | 1538 | Died |
|---|---|---|---|---|---|---|---|---|
| | | | | Visitation | | 29 Sept. | | |
| c1455 | John Gisburne | **Prior** | Prior | d.7 March | | | | 1502 |
| c1465 | William Salinge | scholar/ priest | canon | **Prior** | d.14 March | | | 1520 |
| | Robert Doo | sacristan | | precentor almoner infirmarer | | | | |
| | Godfrey Westminster | canon | | succentor | | | | |
| | John Bardy (Berde) | - | canon | master of novices refectorer | | | | |
| | William Russell | canon | canon | sacristan | | | | |
| 1462 | Andrew Paynell | canon entered 1480 | canon | canon | 3rd prior precentor | | | |
| | John Laborne (Labrum) | - | canon | kitchener sub-cellarer | | | | |
| | Arnold Bynchester | - | canon | warden of lady chapel | | | | |
| 1467 | John Marshall (Mershall) | entered 1483 | canon | canon | canon | | | |
| c1480 | John Lacy | | | professed 1510 | **Prior** | d 16 Jan. | | 1530 |
| c1493 | Thomas Wandsworth | | | canon | (at law school) | kitchener cellarer | Prior of Bodmin | c1549 |
| 1485 | John Sandwyche | | entered 1493 | | kitchener | | | |
| 1490 | John London | | | entered 1503 | canon | | | |
| 1496 | John Ramsey | | | | canon; bachelor of divinity 1522 | **Prior** | prior | 1558 |
| 1494 | John Debnam (Debenham) | | | | subdeacon | infirmarer | subprior | c1558 |
| | Thomas Godmanchester | | | priest 1504 | refectorer | | sacrist | |
| | John Codyngton | | | priest 1513 | canon | sacrist | | 1593 |
| | Richard Wyndsor (Wyndesse, Wydeser) | | | priest 1518 | canon | precentor chanter | | |
| | George Albyn (Abbyn) | | | | canon priest 1523 | warden of lady chapel | succentor | 1557 |
| | John Hayward | | priest | | - | - | canon | |
| | Richard Benese (Benys) | priested at Oxford | | | - | succentor | | 1547 |
| | Thomas Mychell | | | | - | canon | | |
| | Edmund Dowman (Downam) | | | | - | subdeacon | 3rd prior | 1568 |
| | Thomas Paynell (Panell) | | | | - | acolyte | canon | 1564 |
| | John Salyng | | | | - | subdeacon | canon | 1570 |
| | John Martyn | | | | - | subdeacon | canon | |
| | Robert Knyght (Knycht) | | | | acolyte | - | canon priest 1536 | ?1575 |
| | John Page | | | | | - | scholar | |

## Important leases

| Date | Place | Leased to | Term (years) | Source |
|---|---|---|---|---|
| 1516 | Kingston church patronage | certain citizens of London | | Heales p.322 |
| 1518 | East Molesey manor | Sir John Hennege | 66 | Heales p.341 |
| | | | | M & B ii 781 |
| 1520 | *Brickhouse*, Merton | William Lok | 55 | Heales p.329 |
| 1527 | Carshalton church & rectory | William Muschamp | 31 | Heales p.329/330 |
| 1528 | Merton church & rectory | Wm. & Thos Saunder | 40 | Heales p.330 |
| | | (re-leased 1537) | 40 | Heales p.344 |
| 1530 | Tenement in Southwark | Percival Skerne | 41 | Heales p.334 |
| 1532 | Kingston church & rectory | Richard Thomas | 21 | Heales p.334 |
| 1532 | *Merton Holts* | William Lok | 32 | Heales p.335/6 |
| 1533 | Merton Grange (part 1) | John Hillier | 21 | Heales p.336/7 |
| 1533 | Taplow manor | Thomas Manfeld | 21 | Heales p.338 |
| 1534 | Amery Mills, Merton | William Moraunt | 22 | Heales p.338 |
| 1534 | Merton Grange (part 2) | John Hillier | 21 | Heales p.338 |
| 1534 | Chessington manor | Richard Rogers | 21 | Heales p.338 |
| 1534 | Effingham church & rectory | John Holgate | 21 | Heales p.339 |
| 1535 | Kingswood manor | John Kempsall | 40 | Heales p.339 |
| 1535 | Tadworth manor | John Steward | 21 | Heales p.339 |
| 1535 | Little Ashtead manor | John Holgate | 21 | Heales p.339 |
| 1536 | Westbarns, Merton | Thos. & Geoffrey Bedle | 60 | Heales p.342/3 |
| 1536 | *Salyngs*, Merton | John Clerk | 40 | Heales p.341/2/3 |
| 1537 | *Entmore meadow*, Ewell | William Saunders | 80 | Heales p.344 |

*Tile fragments found at Merton priory by Colonel Bidder*
*SAC 38 pt I (1929) p.58 (reproduced by permission)*

# 18. The Beginning of the End

*"What we call the beginning is often the end*
*And to make an end is to make a beginning.*
*The end is where we start from."*
T S Eliot *Four Quartets* 'Little Gidding' V

Following the disaster of the Great Plague in 1348 and the troubles of the Peasants' Revolt of 1381, many monasteries found it difficult to continue a full existence as a religious community and to play a leading part in the countryside. Labour became scarce, the numbers of brethren decreased and the economy contracted.

Discipline within the community became more lax with no compensatory increase of sacramental devotion, or preaching, or works of charity. The canon found the making and decorating of service books demeaning for a priest. Writing was now a common attainment outside the monastery. Teaching was possible for some canons but the lack of a satisfying occupation became a problem throughout the 15th century. The prior retained his position in the community but he no longer lived amongst the canons as one who served.

There was general relaxation of fasting and abstinence, and private ownership and privilege were allowed. All this encouraged a new breed of canons. However, the oblates still arrived at the age of five to seven and received early education. The priory then supported them as they progressed to higher education and many returned to follow their chosen career as a canon of the priory.

On 1 April 1514 Henry VIII confirmed all grants and charters in favour of Merton priory from its foundation to the present, at a charge of 20 marks (£13.33).[329]

## Important Leases

Most monasteries now began to secure immediate value of property in exchange for long leases. Leases contracted by Merton priory included some for over 40 years and one for 80 years. Even the rectorial rights of the appropriated churches of Carshalton, Effingham, Kingston and Merton were leased to laymen (see table on facing page).

The King required the Church to help pay for his expenses in France, and in 1522 Merton priory was assessed at £133 by way of a forced loan. The assessment for the bishop of Winchester was £200.

## The Last Days

In August 1535 Thomas Cromwell appointed auditors to assess the value of monastic spiritualities (income from church tithes, glebe lands, oblations etc.). This operation was known as the *Valor Ecclesiasticus* and Visitors called on every monastery. It was a survey as well as an assessment of value and they examined the title deeds of property and special privileges, observed the maintenance of buildings, investigated the conduct of the brethren, giving opportunity for any who were discontented to speak, and listened to accusations about others. They looked at almsgiving, the keeping of proper accounts and the observing of the Rule. Current valuations were compared with those used to estimate the tenths payable to the authorities. Injunctions were issued that no canon was to leave the precinct, brethren under the age of 20 were to be dismissed and the prior was to exalt the king in a sermon and "attack the power of the pope". Bishops were reduced to silence by a letter from Cromwell in September forbidding any interference.[330] An obscure message informs us that "the Auditors would only meddle with Merton Abbey".[331]

Commissioner Richard Layton visited Merton priory on 27 September 1535 and wrote to Thomas Cromwell informing him that there were 18 fat oxen whereof Sir Nicholas Carew of Beddington, Surrey, wanted part; 40 fat sheep, 200 quarters of malt and £30 in ling and haberdyne (dried and salted cod). Layton asked if Cromwell required any of these things for his own household and if so, would he confirm by the bearer.[332]

The net annual general income for Merton priory shown in the *Valor Ecclesiasticus* was £958, which made it the second richest Augustinian house after Cirencester, a daughter-house of Merton. Most of the income came from tenants (£641) and tithes (£239).

On 10 March 1536, the prior of Merton affirmed that Henry VIII was the supreme head of the Church in England, next after God.

Gradually, after years of uncertainty, many of the canons had become ready for the final dissolution of the monasteries. Being priests, they would find it easy to obtain positions either in a parish or a town fraternity. They would also be released from their vows[333] and could own property.

Many monasteries were "spoiled of their ornaments" before suppression. It would appear that a great part of the damage they received was done under cover of the visitations, before any Dissolution Act had been passed.[334] Many service books were removed – missals with jewelled clasps, graduals, psalters, hymnals, antiphonals etc. In use, the greatest care had been bestowed on them for centuries. Out of use resulted in their immediate desecration.

Prior Ramsey made the journey to London to make a 'privy surrender', and crown agents drafted a deed of surrender. Commissioners empanelled a local jury of 12 trusted men to oversee the compilation of an inventory.

On 16 April 1538 Dr Layton, the king's commissioner, arrived at Merton bearing the prepared form of surrender which was signed by all the canons in their beloved chapter house. Whilst the 15 canons were still 'in residence', the destruction of the priory buildings was already taking place.

On 9 May 1538 Thomas Cromwell signed an order granting the last prior a messuage in London[335] with a pension of 200 marks (£133.33) a year. The canons received from 11 marks (£7.33) per annum upwards, depending on age. Servants were given 'rewards' which consisted of a year's wages.

Thereafter the 'dissolved' canons left Merton bearing their personal bundles, to seek temporary shelter with friends. Soon the final traces of Merton priory were removed and the exact site of the once famous building sank into oblivion and was lost until found by Colonel Bidder's gardener in 1922.

By 1553 the prior and eight canons were still drawing pensions, viz. Thomas Paynell (£10), John Debnam (£8), John Codyngton, John Salying, John Page, George Albyn, Robert Knycht and Thomas Mychell (each receiving £7.33).[336]

*John Ram-*
*sey – prior*
*John Debnam*
*Thomas Godme'-chester*
*John Codyngton*
*Richard Wyndesore*
*George Albyn*
*John Hayward*
*Richard Benese*
*Thomas Mychell*
*Edmund Dowman*
*Thomas Paynell*
*John Salyng*

*John Martyn*
*Robert Knicht*
*John Page*

*Signatures of the last canons of Merton*
*(Photograph reproduced from A Heales* The Records of Merton Priory *(1898)*
*by courtesy of The National Archives: E322/152)*

## The Monastic Treasure

Commissioners were appointed to make valuations of surrendered priories, but in 1538 they were so overwhelmed by the increasing numbers that they often engaged "a retinue of strangers from London"[337] to make valuations.

All church plate was received by the king's Master of the Jewels, Sir John Williams, and valued on weight in ounces. He compiled a check-list of the main inventory from 26 April 1538 until 4 December 1545, which has survived.[338]

He received from Richard Layton, John ap Rice, Edward Carne, Anthony Bellach, John Smith, "Commissioners for the Dissolution of the late Priory of Marten, in the County of Surrey viz. in gold plate v oz. iij $\text{q}^{\text{ært}}$ dï [5 7/8 oz]. In gilt plate Dlvi oz. [556 oz], in parcel gilt and white Dcij oz. [602 oz]. In all, like as by indenture of the xxvjth of April, anno map Regis predict XXIXmo[339] hereupon confirmed and remaining doth appear.

$\text{M}^{\dagger}$clxiij oz. iij $\text{q}^{\text{ært}}$ dï [1163 7/8 oz]."

The first two commissioners mentioned had already visited Merton in 1535 in connection with the *Valor Ecclesiasticus* when they tried unsuccessfully to dismiss ten canons.

### Inventories of the monastic treasure of various houses

Items included sacred vessels such as chalices, censers, jewelled gloves, rings, crucifixes, candlesticks, patens and cruets. The following are a few inventories for comparison with Merton.

| Monastery | 1535 value V.E. * £ | Gold plate oz. | Gilt plate oz. | Parcel Gilt & Silver oz. | Total | Date |
|---|---|---|---|---|---|---|
| **Augustinian** | | | | | | |
| Llanthony | 728 | - | 1,145 | 199 | 1,344 | 26 April 1538 |
| St Barts. London | 693 | - | 591 | 681 | 1,272 | 2 November 1540 |
| Merton | 958 | 6 | 556 | 602 | 1,164 | 26 April 1538 |
| Kenilworth | 539 | - | 686 | 249 | 935 | 26 April 1538 |
| Leicester | 947 | - | 374 | 530 | 904 | 26 April 1538 |
| Southwark | 624 | - | 182 | 407 | 589 | 5 March 1540 |
| Newark | 259 | - | 142 | 169 | 311 | 18 January 1539 |
| Huntingdon | 188 | - | 30 | 60 | 90 | 26 April 1538 |
| **Cluniac** | | | | | | |
| Bermondsey | 46 | - | 176 | 500 | 676 | 7 July 1539 |
| **Benedictine** | | | | | | |
| Glastonbury | 3,311 | 71 | 7,214 | 6,387 | 13,672 | 24 October 1539 |
| St Albans | 2,102 | 122 | 2,990 | 1,134 | 4,246 | 17 December 1539 |

*V.E. = *Valor Ecclesiasticus* – The Commissioners' valuation in 1535

# 19. A Priory Laid Bare

*"These things which you are gazing at – the time will come when not one stone of them will be left upon another."*
Luke 21:5/6

Even as the canons in the chapter house, on 16 April 1538, appended their signatures to the suppression document, builders and carters were converging on Merton from the districts around. There was so much demolition work to be carried out covering an area of some 65 acres (26 ha). Each generation over several centuries had extended and improved their 'city'. There were very many habitable buildings to be razed to the ground. So the builders moved in and the residents moved out. This must have resulted in a clash of human beings and activities, and the 'city' became an 'atro-city'.

Messrs Dickenson and Clement, the master bricklayer and the master carpenter, earlier visitors to the priory (see Prologue), knew what they had to do. They were to remove all the buildings, reclaim useable material, transport it to Cuddington and supply the royal contractors who were now constructing a palace without equal – *nonpareil.*[340]

In May 1538 a single tiler climbed ladders to "uncover the body of the church at Merton Abbey" i.e. removing tiles from the church roof. He was John de Whytaker of Merton who was paid 13s 4d (67p) for so doing. The same man was at Cuddington in July and August where he 'dry laid' 27,000 tiles on the king's barn there, and was paid 9d (4p) per thousand tiles, thus receiving a further £1.

The building accounts show that £184 was spent in 1538 on wages for plumbers.[341] At the priory site, excavations in 1976 between the chapter house and infirmary revealed a clay bowl-like hole containing lead-drops and a possible crucible. This could have been a hearth where lead salvaged from roofs and windows had been melted to form 'pigs'. A lead ingot found in the Dissolution layers may have been part of one. The fires would have been fuelled with old, well-seasoned wood carvings, easily available.

*Possible lead smelting hearth discovered during excavations at Merton priory in 1976 .*
*(Photograph by W J Rudd by permission of the site director)*

Further excavations in 1988 south of the infirmary hall revealed large quantities of window lead, glass and fragments of floor tile from a spread of rubble. This suggests a deliberate sorting of these materials during demolition. Stained glass was not suitable for reuse, with the result that most was destroyed to reclaim the lead that held the glass together.

Bands of workmen travelled from monastery to monastery and were occupied for days or even weeks in melting the covering of roofs, gutters, spouts, pipes and windows into 'pigs' of uneven size. When cool, the pigs were stamped, by the commissioner present, with a Tudor rose surmounted by a crown, and the weight indicated by '1 cwt' (51 kg) circles. These were collected into fothers of 19½ cwt (991 kg). Carters conveyed the fothers along the former Roman road to Cuddington. As each weighed almost a ton it required teams of horses to drag wagons laden with lead. Each fother was worth £4.

When a similar Augustinian monastery at St Osyth, Essex, was demolished in July 1539, it yielded 255 tons (260 tonnes) of lead. Over 100 fothers came from the abbey church, and another 100 from the claustral buildings.

The lead from Merton was well used at Nonsuch. The corner towers and the south front bore decorated plaster panels held in position by wooden beams covered by carved slate hangings and scales of lead. Samuel Pepys visited Nonsuch in 1665 and commented on the walls "covered with Lead and gilded".[342] The octagonal towers had an overhanging storey surmounted by a leaden dome.

As late as 1541, men were still employed at Merton, but now they were sorting material before it was carted to Nonsuch. Only the squared facing stone was sent.[343] This ashlar stone from Merton was used for outer faces of the walls and the masons set the stones so that carvings were hidden. Many pieces of moulding, including a lion gargoyle and a female head were discovered at Nonsuch in 1959. The lion was "carved in the late 15th century … [and] after spending more than four centuries

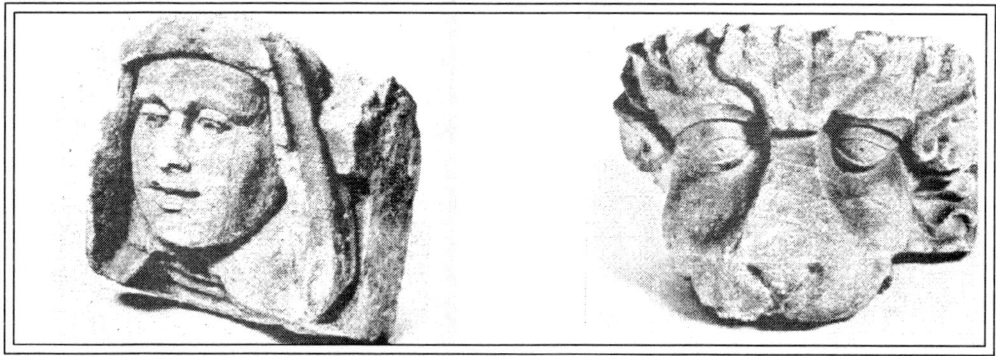

*Female head and lion gargoyle, both from Nonsuch palace, now in the Museum of London (Photographs reproduced from J Dent* The Quest for Nonsuch, *by courtesy of the Nonsuch Palace Excavation Committee and the London Borough of Sutton)*

resting on the flattened top of its head, it was in a remarkably good state of preservation, even its teeth being intact."[344] Next to the lion gargoyle the excavators discovered the 4½ cwt (230 kg) carved roof boss which would have been part of the vaulted roof of the priory church. It is painted red and gilded and was found embedded in the foundations of the south-east tower of the Inner Court at Nonsuch Palace which was probably built in 1543.[345] It would seem that, with the lead covering, Merton priory was present in the south-east tower, from top to bottom.

*'An Impression of Nonsuch' by J Tavenor-Perry, pictured in* Memorials of Old Surrey *1911 p143*

Some stone at the priory would have been used locally and in 1550 stone was supplied to one Thomas Mabson,[346] but soon all above-surface stone had been removed. In 1559 the churchwardens of Battersea paid "14/- [70p] for three loads of stone from Merton and 6d. [5p] to John Tyler for **digging up** the stones we bought".[347] Now only the foundations could produce stone in quantity.

The culmination of the destruction must have been the main tower with its set of bells. We can imagine the thoughts of the witnesses. The familiar view – then the noise of the crash – the clouds of dust – the priory lost to sight. The monument of 400 years of powerful influence was no more.

*Worked stone from Merton priory incorporated in the footings of Nonsuch palace (Photographs by R Miller by permission of the site director, 1959)*

# Epilogue

*"For who ...*
*Left the warm precincts of the cheerful day,*
*Nor cast one longing ling'ring look behind?"*
Thomas Gray *Elegy Written in a Country Churchyard*

This has been a journey of exploration, an attempt to provide a coherent story from records, but the interpretation is partly a matter of faith and partly a personal examination of possibilities. We can only record what is known and many happenings are still unknown to us.

Monasticism was only a part of our Christian heritage. It was only one of the ways to salvation, but it did show the way for meeting the spiritual and general needs of many people near and far. It gave support to those in need, gave education to many, and practised hygiene in living. It gave employment to the populace, improved farming methods, tamed and used rivers, and throughout the centuries encouraged craftsmen and all the arts.

Monasteries were permanent institutions, owning acres of agricultural land, and buildings of brick and stone in towns and the countryside. They were patrons of hundreds of parish churches and lords of many manors. They collected taxes and dispensed justice.

The outlook of monks changed over succeeding generations. By the 15th century monasteries had ceased to be the only seats of learning, and the invention of printing made the laborious copying of manuscripts unnecessary as a monastic industry.

Like a plant, the growth of monasticism was unpredictable. Spurts of development and blossoming followed by withering and decay. There were successes and there were failures, some mutations good, others bad. History consists of past events and no one can undo one moment of them.

The Dissolution of the monasteries gave rise to painful times in the Church for everybody. Henry VIII succeeded in curbing the excessive riches of the Church and acquiring much of it for himself. He was also fighting against the principles of many church leaders who had struggled against their king in fundamental beliefs down the centuries. Men such as Thomas Becket, Edmund Rich, Robert Grosseteste,[348] William of Wykeham, and John Peckham. Henry tried to expunge the name of Becket from history by having his name removed from official records and church dedications.

No doubt the translation of the New Testament into English by William Tyndale in 1526 had a marked effect on attitudes. Banned copies certainly found their way to Merton and some of the canons were leading writers in the vernacular. There was a fresh interpretation of parts of the New Testament – e.g. we are called to repent rather than to do penance (Matthew 4:17). In 1535 Miles Coverdale's bible found its way to Southwark and a new appreciation of the Word led to an appreciation of words. It could be said that the Reformation helped to produce the fine literature which came from Shakespeare, Marlowe and Donne. True, the destruction of the priory meant the loss of works of art, but much of the architecture of the centuries is not lost. We still have our cathedrals which maintain the tradition of daily worship and craftsmanship. We have our universities, and the name of Merton lives on in Oxford. Even the Augustinian hospital foundations of St Bartholomew and St Thomas (Becket) are with us in name.

*Part if the apse of the chapter house 1977*

*North aisle wall of the church 1986*

*(Photographs by W J Rudd by permission of the site director)*

*Flooring slabs in the cloisters 1986*

# Appendix I

## List of the priors of Merton

| No | Name | Dates | | Died |
|---|---|---|---|---|
| 1 | Robert (Bayle) de Tywe | 1117-1150 | | 4 Jan.1150 |
| 2 | Robert | 1150-1167 | | 4 August 1167 |
| 3 | William | 1167-1177 | | 19 February 1177 |
| 4 | Stephen | 1177 | | 6 October 1177 |
| 5 | Robert | 1177-1180 | | 13 May 1180 |
| 6 | Richard | 1180-1198 | | 1 April 1198 |
| 7 | Walter | 1198-1218 | resigned to Chartreuse | Sept.1218 |
| 8 | Thomas de Wllst | 1218-1222 | | <12 Sept.1222 |
| 9 | Giles de Bourne | 1222-1231 | resigned to Beaulieu | 23 Jan. 1231 |
| | | | | September 1231 [349] |
| 10 | Henry de Basing | 1231-1238 | | 22 December 1238 |
| 11 | Robert de Heyham | 1239-1249 | resigned 10 October 1249 | |
| | | Suspended for a few months by papal legate 1244/5 [350] | | |
| 12 | Eustace | 1249-1263 | | 31 January 1263 |
| 13 | Gilbert de Aette (Ashe) | 1263-1292 | | 21 March 1292 |
| 14 | Nicholas de Tregony | 1292-1296 | | 26 September 1296 |
| 15 | Edmund de Herierd | 1296-1305 | excommunicated 1300/1<br>Resigned on 25 September 1305<br>and resided in precinct area | |
| 16 | Geoffrey de Alconbury | 1306-1307 | | 15 March 1307 |
| 17 | William de Brokesborn | 1307-1335 | | early March 1335 |
| 18 | Thomas de Cantia (Kent) | 1335-1339 | | <20 September 1339 |
| 19 | John de Littleton | 1339-1345 | deposed <12 August 1345 | |
| 20 | William Friston | 1345-1361 | | <22 August 1361 |
| 21 | Geoffrey de Chaddesley | 1361-1368 | | 6 October 1368 |
| 22 | Robert de Windsor | 1368-1403 | | 6 May 1403 |
| 23 | Michael Kympton | 1403-1413 | | 20 October 1413 |
| 24 | John de Romeny | 1413-1422 | | 1422 |
| 25 | Thomas Schirfield | 1422-1432 | resigned 1432 | 21 April 1439 |
| 26 | William Kent | 1432-1442 | | 1442 |
| 27 | John Kingston | 1442-1485 | | 2 January 1485 |
| 28 | John Gysburne | 1485-1502 | | 7 March 1502 |
| 29 | William Salynge | 1502-1520 | | 14 March 1520 |
| 30 | John Lacy | 1520-1530 | | 16 January 1530 |
| 31 | John Ramsey | 1530-1538 | | 15 April 1558 |
| | | surrendered priory 16 April 1538 | | |

Average tenure of office – 13 years 6 months

Longest tenure – John Kingston – 42 years 16 days

# Appendix II

## Chronology of important events at Merton priory

| | | |
|---|---|---|
| 1114 | Canons arrive from Huntingdon | p.9 |
| 1117 | New site of priory occupied | 10 |
| *c*.1118 | Nicholas Breakspear being taught at Merton | 29 |
| 1124 | Guy of Merton, schoolmaster, dies | 32 |
| 1125 | Death of Gilbert the founder | 15 |
| 1120-32 | Seven daughter houses founded | 34 |
| 1130 | Thomas Becket being educated at Merton | 29/30 |
| *c*.1155 | Church rebuilt | 17 |
| 1156 | Gift of Ewell manor | 45 |
| *c*.1196 | Enlarged priory completed | 18 |
| 1197 | New silver seal introduced | 18 |
| 1212/3 | Edmund Rich at Merton | 65 |
| 1215 | Runnymede. Letters of safe conduct issued | 73, 86 |
| <1216 | Precinct buildings destroyed by fire | 70 |
| 1217 | Peace terms confirmed at Merton | 73 |
| 1222 | Storm destroys tower at Merton | 113 |
| 1232 | Hubert de Burgh seeks sanctuary | 66 |
| 1236 | Royal Council at Merton | 87 |
| 1241 | New silver seal introduced | 3 |
| 1258 | Convocation at Merton | 91 |
| 1262 | Priory assists Walter de Merton to set up college | 88/89 |
| 1273 | Robert Kilwardby consecrated archbishop at Merton | 91 |
| 1310 | Priory "oppressed with poverty" | 113 |
| 1312 | Knight Templar sent to Merton | 93 |
| *c*.1325 | Presbytery and lady chapel rebuilt | ii |
| 1346 | Prosperity for many | 46 |
| 1376 | William of Wykeham seeks refuge | 67 |
| 1393 | Nave of church and lady chapel requiring repairs | 55 |
| 1395 | Dormitories needing repairs | 41 |
| 1412 | Privy Council at Merton (Henry IV) | 75 |
| 1437 | Henry VI crowned | 75 |
| 1522 | Forced loan. Merton assessed at £133 | 101 |
| 1535 | Commissioner Richard Layton visits priory | 102 |
| 1538 | Surrender and destruction | 2, 102, 105-7 |

# Appendix III

## Disasters – Famine, Fire, Plague and Storm

Droughts and floods ruined crops, caused cattle disease and affected the income of the priory as well as the labourers. Monasteries such as Merton planned long-term and were able to demonstrate rational solutions to many natural catastrophes. Regular hedging and ditching were essential to protect farms and gardens from wind, rain and floods. Building in stone was a better safeguard against fire than traditional timber structures. Floods could sometimes be controlled by constructing dikes and fitting sluices. Flood plains could be maintained.

The large monastic barns in the countryside granges protected communities from many famines and plagues.

| Date | Disaster |
|---|---|
| 1118 May 1 | Death of queen Maud following her visit to Merton with prince William, (Heales p.4) |
| 1120 | Loss of the White Ship and prince William. "a severe blow to the convent" |
| 1124 | Famine and drought "which killed many thousands" (Colker (70) pp.244-6; *Anglo Saxon Chronicle* s.a.1124) |
| 1133 | Fire in London. Gilbert Becket's house destroyed |
| 1136 | Fire in London |
| 1161 | Fire in London |
| 1165 | Earthquake in southern England |
| 1203 | Bad harvest after flood. (Waverley annals) |
| 1208-14 | Interdict of England |
| 1212 | Fire in London. Eastern arm of Southwark priory destroyed<br>Thatched roofs in London banned. Most henceforth tiled<br>(J Schofield *The Buildings of London from Conquest to Gt. Fire* 1993.) |
| <1216 | Fire in Merton priory precinct. (Heales p.71) |
| 1222 Dec. | Severe storms. Collapse of Merton's tower.(Dunstable annals iii 76) |
| 1243 June | Tempest in Merton. (Heales p.112) |
| 1251 | Drought for four months. Hay crop reduced by half, loss of cattle |
| 1257/8 | Severe winter. Famine in London |
| 1274-1301 | Sheep disease (murrain) for twenty-eight years |
| 1294 Oct. | Major floods in Southwark |
| 1310 | "manifestly oppressed with poverty". (Heales p.202.) |

| | |
|---|---|
| 1316 | Great Famine |
| 1317 | Famine in London |
| 1322 | Great Famine |
| 1348-50 | Black Death |
| 1360-62 | *Secunda pestic.* Wm. Friston, prior of Merton died of plague August 1361. |
| 1368-69 | Plague. Prior Geoffrey de Chaddesley died 6 October 1368. (*VCH* I p.361) |
| 1379 | Plague |
| 1387 Sept. | "some dwellings…in deficient repair and need". (Heales pp.269/70) |
| 1387-93 | "murrain in manors for six years …" (Heales p.284) |
| 1394 | "… now the tempest has ceased …" (Heales p.287) |
| c1395 | "losses of cattle by pestilence … dormitories ready to fall". (Heales p.287; H Salter *Chapters of the Augustinian Canons* 1922 p.176) |
| 1405-7 | Plague |
| 1439 | Plague |
| 1445 | Kingston town fire |
| 1478 | Plague |
| 1480 | Poor harvest |
| 1484/5 | English Sweat (probably a virus disease). In London three sheriffs and three mayors died. |
| 1500-2 | Plague |
| 1519 | Dean Colet (founder of St Paul's school in 1509) died of "pestilential sweating". (Heales p.323) |
| 1520 | Plague and poor harvest |
| 1527/8 | Plague, famine. Sweating sickness April - June 1528 |
| 1535-39 | Plague |
| 1538 | Destruction of priory buildings by Henry VIII |

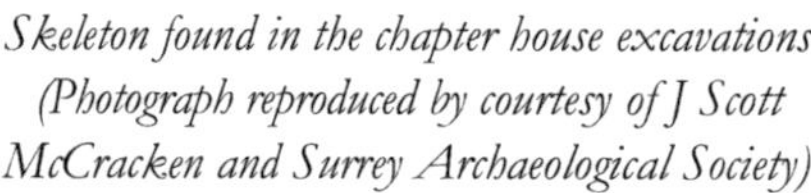

*Skeleton found in the chapter house excavations (Photograph reproduced by courtesy of J Scott McCracken and Surrey Archaeological Society)*

# Appendix IV

## Unreliable Evidence

*"To err is human; to forgive, divine."*
Alexander Pope *An Essay on Criticism*

Every author will endeavour **not** to make mistakes, but no publication is ever completely free of errors. For any discovered, please forgive.

Looking at previous histories of Merton priory, it is apparent that published 'facts' are not always from original sources. Even those from original sources need careful thought with backing from alternative sources.

*"Who shall decide when doctors disagree,*
*And soundest casuists doubt, like you and me?"*
Alexander Pope *Epistle* iii. – 'To Lord Bathurst'

Below are listed some misleading statements made about the priory, which are so often copied from publication to publication, sometimes down the centuries.

1. Gilbert the founder did **not die in 1130**. He died in 1125, and the *Historia Fundationis* shows the correct date in Roman numerals MCXXV.
2. The statement that "the inhabitants had nowhere to bury their dead" does **not appear in the *Historia Fundationis***.
3. There is **no record** that the founder was buried in the cloister, or that "there was a monument to his memory". There may have been a stone coffin with lid in the church but the location is not known. See Heales p.7.
4. Gilbert did **not become a canon or retire to the priory**. He was active as sheriff of three counties until he died near St Neots, Huntingdon.
5. The canons were **not inducted in 1136 by the bishops of St David and Rochester**. Merton canons were inducted into **Dover** priory by these bishops.
6. The body of Henry I did **not lie in state at Merton** on its journey from Dover to Reading in January 1136.
7. The building of the priory in stone was **not started in 1130**. This began in 1125.
8. Queen Eleanor, wife of Henry III, was **not crowned at Merton**. The coronation took place at Westminster abbey.
9. The church of Cahagnes in Normandy was given to the priory. This was **not Cheam, Surrey.** See page 48.
10. Merton was always a priory and **not an abbey**. Its importance meant that some referred to it as an abbey even before the Dissolution.

*Lt. Col. Harold F Bidder*

*Photograph taken in 1927, during Bidder's excavations, showing detail of flooring within the retrochoir of the church, alongside Station Road. (Reproduced by courtesy of Merton Library and Heritage Service)*

*Memorial plaque unveiled by Colonel Bidder in July 1959.*
*The site is now covered by the Savacentre car park, but the (broken) plaque survives in the chapter house.*

# Monastic Glossary

| | |
|---|---|
| **acolyte** | brother in minor orders but not yet ordained; church official attending a priest |
| **advowson** | right of presentation of a parson to a benefice |
| **appropriation** | taking over of a benefice, resulting in a non-resident rector, with a perpetual vicar installed |
| **benefice** | church living or its property |
| **canon** | brother living according to a Rule; a church decree; the principal part of the Mass |
| **capacities** | dispensation to leave monastery and serve as clergyman in a parish |
| **cartulary** | register of title deeds and charters of privileges |
| **chantry** | endowment for singing masses for donor |
| **claustral** | relating to the cloister |
| ***congé d'élire*** | royal licence to elect a prelate |
| **consuetudinal** | see customary |
| **convent** | religious community living together, (not necessarily women) |
| **corrodian** | pensioner, usually living within the community |
| **crosier/crozier** | a crook carried by a 'mitred abbot' to signify that the prelate should seize and correct the bad and give support to the weak |
| **customary** | customs and observances set down for each monastic community |
| **endowment** | regular provision of income from land tithes, glebe rents or offerings |
| **episcopacy** | bishops of the Church |
| **feudal** | relating to landholding in return for service to the manorial lord |
| **frankalmoign** | land producing income, granted to a monastery to support a chantry |
| **garderobe** | toilet within a building |
| **horarium** | daily time-table of a monastery |
| **incumbent** | clergyman holding a benefice |
| **necrology** | list of deceased benefactors and brethren of house who were being prayed for, also including departed members of kindred monasteries |
| **noviciate/novitiate** | period of probation before taking vows |
| **obedientiary** | monastic departmental officer (under a superior) |
| **oblate** | persons, usually children, dedicated to monastic life |
| **patron** | person possessing right of patronage or advowson |
| **pension** | (after 1185) amount paid by an incumbent to the patron in lieu of tithe |
| **perpetual vicar** | incumbent with security of tenure receiving specified portion of church revenue or a fixed income |
| **pittances** | (*pitantia*) additional dishes at meals and privileges |
| **praemunire** | accepting papal law and not the royal law |
| **presentation** | right of supplying a parson to a benefice |
| **pulpitum** | a deep screen that closed the west end of the choir (see page 55) |
| **secular** | anyone not following monastic vows |
| **seized** | in legal possession of estate especially at time of death |
| **simony** | sale of church appointments or not filling vacancies (Simon Magus – Acts viii) |
| **stipend** | salary paid to a clergyman for duties performed |
| **tithe** | annual payment of 1/10th of the value of goods for the upkeep of clergy and church, payable in cash or kind |
| **votive** | in fulfilment of vow |

## Original Sources of Information

College of Arms, London Arundel MS 28 ff 1-13, 112 – *Historia Fundationis.* Early 15th-cent. document transcribed from an earlier narrative. Circumstantial account of the foundation and the founder.

Brit. Lib. Royal MS 8E ix ff 93 – 98 – The Life of Guy of Merton… 1132x51. A biography by Rainald of Merton.

PRO Cart. Antiq. U.5 ff c 52/20 – The Foundation Charter 1121 – Grant of the ville of Merton to the priory.

Brit. Lib. Cott. MS Cleop. C vii ff 58 - 70. 13th cent. copy – The cartulary of the priory. A vellum volume with 525 deeds. Early records missing as numbering begins at No.39 (f 81).

Bodl. Lib., Oxford Laud. Misc. MS 723. ff 24 -73 – c1400. The Annals of the priory. 200 folio pages of chronicles, visitations by bishop, Kalendar from 1216 to 1441 and certain priory accounts.

Coll. of Arms, London Arundel MS 23 – Extracts from the register of the priory.

Corpus Christi Coll. Cantab. MS 59 ff151-180 – early 14th-century Kalendar Register recording chief events in a calendar from 1065 to 1242.

Sources of information which cannot be traced include the Customary, Necrology, Account Rolls and Dissolution Inventory.

### Abbreviations

| | |
|---|---|
| BL | British Library |
| Colker (69) | M L Colker 'The Life of Guy of Merton' in *Medieval Studies* 31 (1969) Toronto |
| Colker (70) | M L Colker 'Latin Texts concerning Gilbert, Founder of Merton Priory' (*Studia Monastica*, (Abadia de Montserrat, Barcelona), xii) (1970) |
| Dickinson (50) | J C Dickinson *Origins of the Austin Canons…*(1950) |
| Dickinson (51) | J C Dickinson 'English Regular Canons and the Continent' in *Transactions of the Royal Historical Society* 5th series Vol I (1951). |
| Heales | A Heales *Records of Merton Priory* (1898) |
| M & B | Manning & Bray *History of Surrey* Vol. I (1804), Vol. III (1814) |
| MHS | Merton Historical Society |
| MoLAS | Museum of London Archaeology Service. |
| *Mon Ang* | W Dugdale *Monasticon Anglicanum* ed. J Caleys, H Ellis & B Bandinel (1830) |
| PRO | National Archives formerly Public Record Office. |
| *SAC* | *Surrey Archæological Society Collections* |
| SHC | Surrey History Centre, Woking. |
| *VCH* | *Victoria County History: Surrey* (1902) |
| WAM | Westminster Abbey Muniments |

# NOTES AND REFERENCES

## Prologue

1 T Fuller *Church History of Britain* 1655 p.306
2 J Stow *Survey of London* 1603 (ed. Kingsford 1908 I p.142)
3 T Wright *Letters Relating to the Suppression of the Monasteries.* Camden Soc. 26 (1843) p.181; W St J Hope in *Archaeological Journal* 41 (1884) p.6
4 H Braun *English Abbeys* 1971 p.234
5 PRO E 36/245 p.253
S Thurley *Royal Palaces of Tudor England* 1993 p.110
6 J Dent *The Quest for Nonsuch* 1981 p.38
7 *ibid* p.261
8 PRO Exchequer Accounts E 101/477/12
9 Dent *op. cit.* pp.42 & 80
10 PRO E 101/477/12

## Introduction

11 *eremia* - desert
12 Acts ii 44/5; iv 32-35, by Luke the physician and historian
13 Dickinson (50) p.42
14 Dickinson (51) p.71
15 Dickinson (50) p.128
16 *ibid.* p.103n4
Dickinson (51) p.71
17 Dickinson (50) p.103
18 J W Clark (Ed) *Liber Memo. de Eccles. de Bernwella* 1907 p.41
19 C N L Brooke & G Kier *London 800-1216: The Shaping of a City* 1975 p.205
20 C N L Brooke in Beales & Best (eds.) *History, Society and the Churches* 1985 p.56

## 1. Gilbert the Founder

21 Heales p.1
22 J Morris (Ed) *Domesday Book: Surrey* 1975 30b.5
23 Heales p.2
24 *ibid.* p.3
25 D Lysons *Environs of London* I 1792 p.339
26 Colker (70) pp.242 & 250
Heales p.3
27 Lysons *op. cit.* p.340
28 Colker (70) p.242
29 Lysons *op. cit.* p.340
30 Colker (70) p.251
31 E J Kealey *Roger of Salisbury: Viceroy of England* 1972 (California Univ.) p.120
Colker (70) p.243
32 Dickinson (50) p.130
33 PRO Cart. Antiq. U 5 f 52/20
*Mon Ang* vi p.247
34 It was probably the very high status of the witnesses that led J H Round to suspect that the charter of 1121 was a forgery.
35 Heales p.4
36 *ibid.* p.5
37 Colker (70) pp.262/3

## 2. Gilbert the Norman

38 His mother was still active in 1117 (Colker (70) p.244) and therefore unlikely to be of childbearing age before 1066.
39 D Lysons *Environs of London* I, 1792 p.341
40 *Anglo-Saxon Chronicle* s.a.1085
41 P Coss *The Knight in Medieval England 1000-1400* 1993 pp.9/10
42 Heales p.5
43 C Given-Wilson *The Royal Household & the King's Affinity* 1986 pp.7-8
44 *Cartularium Monasterii de Rameseia* (Ramsey Cartulary) I p.238
45 Christopher Brooke suggests that the combination formed a narrow ring around Hugh of Buckland's territory. C Brooke & G Kier *London 800-1216; the Shaping of a City* (Secker & Warburg) 1975 p.205
46 Heales p.2
47 Colker (70) p.244
48 Dickinson (50) p.129
49 Camb. Univ. Library Addtl MS 3021 f.419r
50 WAM 82 & 83
51 Colker (70) p.244
Dickinson (50) p.130
52 Colker (70) p.244/5
The famine is mentioned in the *Anglo-Saxon Chronicle* s.a. 1124.
53 Colker (70) p.245
54 Heales p.5
For Serlo see also chapter 7
55 E J Kealey *Roger of Salisbury: Viceroy of England* 1972 p.120
Colker (70) p.243/4
56 Colker (70) p.246

## 3. Early Buildings

57 Colker (70) p.251
Heales pp.3/4
58 J Harvey *Cathedrals of England & Wales* (Batsford) 1974 p.59
59 J C Robertson *Materials for the History of Thomas Becket* 1878 (RS 67) III p.23

60 Eirike Magnuson (Ed) *Thómas Saga Erkibyskups* (R.S.65) 1875 I p.85
W L Warren *Henry II* 1973 p.455
61 Heales p.21
62 PRO Exch. King's Remembrancer Misc. 1/1b line 58; *English Historical Review* 28 (1913) p.223. *"Prior et conventus de Mertuna xl marcas super vineum in Sudtuna in Surred"*
63 Heales p.22/23
For examples of the king's munificence see *SAC* 71 (1977) p.96
64 Heales p.26
65 *ibid.* p.49/50 (with the last date corrected)
66 *ibid.* p.60

## 4. Augustinian Canons

67 J W Clark *Observances at the Augustinian Priory of Barnwell* (Macmillan & Bowes) 1897 p.133
68 *ibid* p.203
69 D Knowles *The Religious Orders in England* 1950 ii p.229
70 J R H Moorman *Church Life in England in the 13th Century* 1945 p.260
71 H E Salter *Chapters of the Augustinian Canons* (Canterbury & York Society) 1922 p.9. This met at Leicester under the presidency of the prior of Merton.
72 D Knowles *The Monastic Orders in England* 1949 p.361n
73 Heales p.268
74 Salter *op. cit.* p.xxvi
75 Winchester Obedientiary Rolls pp.307ff
76 Heales p.204
77 *ibid.* p.60
78 Daniel 9: 3. "I turned to the Lord God and pleaded with him … in sackcloth and ashes".
79 Hence a dirge was the name for a burial song.
80 *Current Archæology* No.162 Vol.XIV (April 1999) p.237
Bones studied by MoLAS
81 Disseminated Idiopathic Skeletal Hyperostosis (DISH)
Tony Waldron 'DISH at Merton Priory: Evidence for a 'new' occupational disease', *British Medical Journal* 291 (21-28 Dec 1985) pp.1762/3.

## 5. The Prior

82 Heales p.154
83 *ibid.* p.34
84 F M Stenton *Norman London* 1934 p.55
85 *Sussex Archaeological Collections* 7 (1854) p.213
86 Colker (70) p.266
87 Heales p.77
88 The example of Merton in Southwark, was followed by the abbess of Malling (c1200), monasteries at Canterbury, St Augustine and Christchurch (1215), Battle (*c.*1225), Beaulieu (1274), Lewes (*c.*1277), St Swithun, Winchester (1299), Hyde abbey (1305), Waverley (1309), Totnes (1432).
89 Heales pp.233-5, 303-6, 311-4, 324-8
90 M&B I, 252
91 Heales p.319

## 6. Centre of Learning

92 D Knowles *The Historian and Character and other essays* (CUP) 1963 p.195
93 *ibid.* p.194
94 Nicholas' education at Merton was first suggested by R L Poole in *Essays in Medieval History to T F Tout* 1925 p61
95 A Kippis *Biographica Britannica* 1778 I p 64. See also MHS *Bulletin* 129 (March 1999) p.4
96 Collector of wharf dues, beach market tolls etc
97 Dickinson (50) pp.111 n4 and 115
98 Colker (70) p.251
Heales p.3
99 Knowles *op. cit.* p.101
100 Wm fitzStephen *Materials for the History of Thomas Becket* (RS 67) 1875 III 14
101 F Barlow *The English Church 1066-1154* 1979 p.221
102 W Dugdale *Monasticon Anglicanum* 1830 vi pt.1 pp.79/80
103 A M Woodcock (Ed) *Cartulary of St Gregory, Canterbury* in Royal Hist. Soc. 1956 p x
104 Heales p.268
105 H E Salter *Chapters of the Augustinian Canons* (Canterbury & York Soc.) 1922 pp.xxxvii, 239
106 Heales p.90 and 117
107 Colker (69) p.252
Dickinson (50) p.187
108 'Ex historiae Francicae fragmento' in *Recueil des historiens des Gaules et de France* XII (1781) p.3
Colker (69) p.250
Dickinson (50) p.187 n7
109 Colker (69) p.254
110 *ibid.* p.252
111 *ibid.* p.253
112 *ibid.* p.259
113 F Barlow *The English Church 1066-1154* 1979 p.233
114 Colker (69) p.254, 259
If 15 May was the vigil of the Ascension it could only be 1124. (M Brett *The English Church under Henry I* 1975 p.9n.)
115 Colker (69) p.254

## 7. Daughter Houses

116 Heales p.5
117 Colker (70) p.243
118 *ibid.* p.242
119 *ibid.* p.243
D Lysons *Environs of London* I, 1792 p.341
120 Colker (69) p.259
M Brett *The English Church under Henry I* 1975 p.9n
121 Dickinson (50) p.118
122 Further information is contained in *Daughter Houses of Merton Priory* published by the MHS April 2002.

## 8. The Monastic Day

123 When only eight hours of daylight, each 'Hour' was 8/12 or 2/3 of an hour.
124 Three psalms at each 'Hour' meant 21 psalms each day, plus introductory psalms sung at vigils.
125 J W Clark (ed) *The Observances in use at Barnwell Priory* Macmillan & Bowes 1897 p.lxxxv
126 Heales p.325
127 Augustinian Rule. See Migne *Patrologiae cursus; S Augustin Epistolarum* II p.958
128 Dickinson (50) p.182
129 Silence was a sign of obedience and humility. It was likened to an artificial desert to instil solitude amid a crowd.

## 9. Administration Within

130 Dickinson (50) p.159
*Mon Ang* 419a; "*..secundum ordinem beati Augustini et institutionem ecclesiae sancte Marie de Meretune*".
131 Heales p.318
132 *ibid.* p.195
133 *ibid.* p.212/3
134 *ibid.* p.268
135 *ibid.* p.271
136 *ibid.* p.309/310
137 *ibid.* p.318-21
138 C R Cheney *From Becket to Langton* (Manchester University Press) 1956 p.176n
139 D Knowles *The Monastic Order* 1949 p.618
140 Heales p.317
141 H E Salter *Chapters of the Augustinian Canons* (Canterbury & York Soc.) 1922 p. xxxvii
142 *ibid.* p.176
Heales p.287
Chapter met in 1395
143 Salter *op. cit.* pp 104,108
Oseney Acts of Chapter s.a. 1443
144 Heales p.317
Augmentation Office Charters F 27
145 *Book of Common Prayer.* Holy Communion – prayer for the Church militant
146 Heales p.133
147 *ibid.* p.230/1
148 *ibid.* p.233
149 *ibid.* p.248/9
150 *ibid.* p.274;
*Register Wykeham* fo.182
151 Heales p.33
152 Salter *op. cit.* pp.22/3

## 10. Administration Without

153 D Wilkins *Concilia Magnae Britanniae* 1737 Vol.1 p.587
154 R R Tighe & J E Davis *Annals of Windsor* 1858 I p. 340/1
155 Heales p.187
156 Much of Cahagnes, including its church, was destroyed in 1944.
157 Heales p.342
158 "store it in the grange" ? barn – Heales p.33
159 Luke de Hardres bought the right of presentation to a canonry at Merton in about 1177. (Heales p.31)
160 Heales p.284

## 11. The Precinct

161 MHS *Bulletin* 138 (2001) p.4
162 see S F Hockey (Ed) 'The Account-book of Beaulieu Abbey' in Camden Society 16 (1975) pp.182-4
163 Rose Graham in G Barraclough *Social Life in Early England* 1960 p.68
164 *Curia* mentioned until early 14th century. Heales pp.71, 82, 113, 212
165 D Knowles *The Historian and Character and other essays* (CUP) 1963 p.207
166 *Medieval Archaeology* 45 (2001) p.277
167 The Gatehouse site would not provide this view.
168 P J Huggins 'Monastic grange…Waltham Abbey 1970-72' in *Trans. Essex Arch. Soc.* 3rd Series IV (1972)
169 Heales pp.193-5
170 *ibid.* p.238
171 Stone benches were provided inside the walls of the nave, the chapter house, guesthouse and even certain gateways.
172 Heales p.14
173 G G Coulton *Five Centuries of Religion* 1923 I p.142
174 W Lambarde *Topographical Dictionary* 1730 p.212
175 Heales p.284

176 In 1485 William London was custodian (Heales p.303), "of the great chapel…within the church of the monastery" (Heales 306.) A *custos* still existed in 1536 (Heales pp.342, 343.)
177 Heales p.303
178 D Knowles *The Historian & Character and other essays* (CUP) 1963 p.192
179 *ibid.* p.193
180 Examples at Barnwell, Baswick, Felling, Flitcham, Frithelstock, Michelham, Poughley, Shulbrede, Stone, Thurgarton and Warbleton
181 Heales p.332
182 J Raine *The Rites of Durham* (Surtees Soc. 15 1842 p.76)
J T Fowler (Surtees Soc. 107 1903 p.90)
183 PRO Close Rolls 42 Hen III m 14, 1256-9 p.168
John completed the nave vault of Gloucester cathedral by 1245 and went on to build the palace apartments at Guildford with glass windows. Following Merton's chimney repair, John did likewise in the king's chamber at Westminster Palace. In May 1259 over 15 cwt. of stone was delivered from Chaldon quarry. (H M Colvin *Building Accounts of Henry III* (1971) pp.290, 296, 342). John died in 1260.
184 Heales p.305
185 H E Salter *Chapters of the Augustinian Canons* (Canterbury & York Soc.) 1922 p.26
186 *SAC* 36 (1927) p.41
187 The bolting hutch was a large tub containing flour which had been 'bolted' to separate the husks of ground wheat.
188 J W Clark (Ed) *The Observances in use at Barnwell Priory* (Macmillan & Bowes) 1897 p.203
189 *ibid* p.187
190 Heales p.212
191 Pevsner & Nairn *Surrey* 1971 p.363
It was re-erected in 1935 at the parish church.
192 *Medieval Archaeology* 45 (2001) p.277
193 *London Archaeologist* Vol.10 No7 (2003) p.196
194 *Gentleman's Magazine* CCLVI Jan. 1884 p.66 and E Walford *Greater London* Vol 2 (1883-4) p.519
195 Pipe roll 25 Hen III rot. 16d.
This would have been in the south-east, giving access to the drovers' track to the sheep enclosures on Carshalton Downs via Ravensbury and Green Wrythe Lane.
196 Heales p.71, 82, 168, 189, 193/4

## 12. Hospitality

197 Interdict – the prohibition of church services by decree
198 W Wallace *Life of St Edmund of Canterbury* 1893 p.93
199 C C C Cambridge MS lix
Heales p.104,105
200 *ibid.* p.139
201 *ibid.* pp.132/3,137, 162
202 *ibid.* p.179
203 *ibid.* p.158
204 *ibid.* pp.163/4
205 *ibid.* p.165
206 *ibid.* p. 164
207 *ibid.* p.329
*Letters & Papers Henry VIII* iv pt. 1 pp.676, 821, 1053
208 Heales p.62
J Blair *Early Medieval Surrey* (Sutton) 1991 p.99
209 Heales p.170
210 *ibid.* p.284
211 *ibid.* p.71
212 *ibid.* p.168
213 *ibid.* p.204
214 G H Fowler *Dunstable Charters* Bedfordshire Historical Society (1926) p.228
215 Heales p.245
*VCH* 2 p.97
216 Record Office Calendar iii 248, iv pt 3 p.2810
217 *bona cervisia.* Not standard convent beer or *debili cervisia* (weak beer)
218 Heales p.164
219 Cart. Rot. 36 Hen III m11
Heales p.124
220 Heales p.269
221 Cal. Patent Roll 19 Edw. I m10 p.54
20 Edw. I m5 p.55
Heales p.173
222 Close Roll 36 Hen III m14
Heales p.125

## 13. Royal Visitors

223 Colker (70) p.243
D Lysons *Environs of London* I, 1792 p.340
Heales p.2
224 Heales pp. 40/41
225 Pipe Roll 9 Henry II vi p.62
*SAC* 71 (1977) p.98
226 Heales p.60
227 MHS *Bulletin* No 127 (Sept. 1998) pp.8/9
228 Patent Rolls 17 John m 22 p.145
Heales pp.70/72, with incorrect years
229 *SAC* 36 (1925) p.53
230 MHS *Bulletin* No. 138 (2001) pp14-16
231 Patent Rolls 30 Hen.III m5

232 D Williamson *Kings and Queens of Britain* 1991 p.72
233 J Hunter 'Journal of the mission of Isabella …' in *Archaeologia* 36 (1855) p.257
MHS *Bulletin* 148 (June 2004)
234 *Archaeologia* 31 (1850) p.43
Heales p.248;
MHS *Bulletin* 141 (March 2002) p.9
235 Heales p.296
N H Nicholas *Privy Council of England, Proceedings* … II (1834) p.38
236 Heales p.298
237 *ibid.* p.336

## 14. Endowments

238 O Vital *Historia Ecclesiastica* Book XI 2 (Chibnall VI 1978 p.16/17)
239 W H Frere 'The early history of the canons regular…' in *Fasciculus J W Clark dicatus* 1909 pp.193, 216
240 J Blair *Early Medieval Surrey* (Sutton) 1991 p.99.
241 Colker (70) p.243
242 Heales pp.9/10
Cluia was Kingscliffe.
243 Blair *op. cit.* p.124
*VCH* 3 pp.321-5
244 Heales p.15
245 *ibid.* p.153
246 *ibid.* p.62

## 15. A Local Landlord

247 College of Arms Arundel MS 28, section I:19 from Colker (1970), pp. 241-271
248 Heales p.135
249 *VCH* iv, 65 – De Banco R. 355, m. 172; 354, m. 50 d. (East. 22 Ed. III)
250 *VCH* ii, 99 – Anct. Pet. 3007. No date is given for this petition, but a William de Kent became prior in 1439, having previously been sub-prior. However, the name was not uncommon – a former canon of Merton, William de Cantia, on 3rd June 1258 "without the consent of the Prior and Convent, entered secretly, intending with great temerity to reform the place and arrangements", but was banished to another monastery of the Order.
251 Heales p.296.
252 Merton Court Rolls – Guildhall Library ms 34, 100/205
253 Ministers Accounts – PRO SC 6/Hen VIII/3463 m5
254 *ibid* – mm5 & 18
255 WAM Book 11, fo. 169v;
Heales p.101 quoting *Pedes finium* 21 Hen III, Surrey, No.209
256 WAM 27295-27305
257 Ministers Accounts – PRO SC 6/Hen VIII/3463 m9
258 *ibid* m19
259 *ibid* m15
260 *ibid* m31
261 Heales p.297-8
*VCH* iii, 502
262 Ministers Accounts – PRO SC 6/Hen VIII/3463 m33
Heales 64
263 *ibid* m17
264 *ibid* m28
265 Ministers Accounts – PRO SC 6/Hen VIII/3463 m26
WAM Book 11, fo 370
266 Heales p.20
267 Ministers Accounts – PRO SC 6/Hen VIII/3463 m11
268 *ibid* m7
269 Deedes, C (ed) *Register or Memorial of Ewell* (1913) 166-169
270 Ministers Accounts – PRO SC 6/Hen VIII/3463 m20
271 *ibid* m33
272 *ibid* m31
273 *ibid* m32
274 Heales pp340-341
275 *ibid.* p.257
*VCH* iv, 122
276 Lambert, H C M *History of Banstead in Surrey* I (1912), 130-135, 353-356
277 *VCH* iv, 94
278 Ministers Accounts – PRO SC 6/Hen VIII/3463 m25
279 *ibid* m27
280 *ibid* m15
281 See note 62. No further references to this vineyard are extant, but the Merton court rolls refer to a tenement called "Blakewaters in Sutton" in 1516-1517 – Guildhall Library ms 34, 100/205
282 *VCH Middlesex* ii, 267; vii, 82, 136
*VCH Surrey* iv, 70
Heales 106, 108, 251-3, 260-3, 285-6, 295-6
283 Ministers Accounts – PRO SC 6/Hen VIII/3463 m15
284 *ibid* m13

## 16. A Glimpse of Greatness

285 Eirike Magnuson (Ed) *Thómas Saga Erkibyskups* (R.S.65) 1875 I p.85
W L Warren *Henry II* 1973 p.455. "he took on a black cape and a white surplice which go with the ordination of a canon regular, and this rule he followeth out afterward".
286 *Radulphi de Diceto Opera Historica* (RS 68) II p.88
287 *Henry Knighton Chronicon* (RS 92) I p.167
Heales p.48
288 *SAC* 36 (1925)p.48
289 Further information is contained in MHS *Bulletin* 127 (1998) pp.8/9
290 C L Kingsford in the *Dictionary of National Biography*, OUP 1997 Vol. 13 p.299
291 Surrey Eyre (October 1235), Nos.61 and 190
292 F M Powicke *King Henry III and Lord Edward* 1947 I p.308
293 Heales p.142
294 *ibid.* p.186
295 Colker (70) p.243
296 Heales p.91
297 *ibid.* p.154
298 *ibid.* p.156
299 PRO Special Collection 1-18/169
300 Heales p.133,134 & 197
301 Further information is contained in MHS *Bulletin* 144 (2002) pp.12/13
302 D Wilkins *Concilia Magnae Britanniae* ii 1737 p.279
303 Close Roll Cal. pp.14,49
*SAC* 22 (1909) p.156/7
304 *SAC* 22 (1909) p.157
305 Bermondsey priory held the superior rights. *SAC* 16 (1901) p.561
306 *Sussex Archaeological Collections* 9 (1857) p.274; *English Historical Review* Vol. 24 (1909) p.441
307 Heales p.212; *VCH* ii p.98
*Sussex Archaeological Collections* 9 (1857) p.272
308 *VCH* ii p.98; Bull of pope John XXII
309 Heales p.207
310 In 1381 Wycliffe denied the doctrine of transubstantiation. His view was consubstantiation i.e. that the bread and wine was not replaced by the body of Christ but that He was present with it.
311 Bodl. MS 723 (Merton Chronicle)
D Lysons *Environs of London* I, 1792 p.341
312 Heales p.292; BL.Cole MS 44 p.358
313 Heales p.295
314 S Brigden *London and the Reformation* 1989 p.57
315 BL copy – ref.C40e36
316 *Royal Historical Letters of Henry III* I p.100
317 Annals of Waverley; Heales p.112
318 *Annales Monastici* (Waverley) II p.240
319 Heales p.58

## 17. Pastures New

320 Dickinson (50) p.195
321 J W Clark *The Observances in Use … at Barnwell* (Macmillan & Bowes) 1897 p.32
322 *Annales Monastici* (Waverley abbey) ii p.290
323 Heales p.191
324 *ibid.* p.234
325 *ibid.* p.294
326 *ibid.* p.303 & 309
327 *SAC* 52 (1952) p.34
328 Calendar of Papal Register 1492-95 Vol.16 No. 575

## 18. The Beginning of the End

329 Heales p.322
330 *Letters & Papers of Henry VIII* ix 517
331 *ibid* Cal. ix p.2; Heales p.339
332 *ibid* Henry VIII xiii (1) 7/83-5
*VCH* 2 p.101
333 As provided for under the law of 1536
334 A Amos *Observations on the Statutes of the Reformation Parliament of Henry VIII* 1859 p.309,
335 'Prior's house' Trinity Lane, south of Holy Trinity the Little
336 Browne Willis *An history of the mitred parliamentary abbies (sic)* … 1719 II p.231
337 M E C Walcott 'Inventories & valuations of religious houses' in *Archaeologia* xliii (1871) pp.202 & 229
338 W B D D Turnbull (ed.) *Account of the Monastic Treasures* … Abbotsford Club 1836 p.11
339 The 29th regnal year ended on 22 April 1538, the correct year for the date of suppression but not of the indenture.

## 19. A Priory Laid Bare

340 J Dent *The Quest for Nonsuch* 1981 p.38
341 *ibid.* p.47
342 S Pepys *Diary* 21 Sept 1665
343 Dent *op. cit.* 1981 p.80
344 *ibid.* p.101; *Daily Telegraph* 9 Sept. 1959 p.14. The carvings are on display in the Museum of London.
345 *SAC* 58 (1961) p.3
346 SHC (former SRO 281/2/18)
347 Battersea Churchwardens' Accounts f.2a p.236

## Epilogue

348 Grosseteste, bishop of Lincoln, died in 1253, and it was at the convocation at Merton in 1258 that his complaints against the pope and the king were aired. (See MHS *Bulletin* 144 (Dec 2002) p.13.)

## Appendix I

349 Surrey Record Society Vol. 32 (1983) p.475
350 Matthew Paris *Chron. Major.* iv 284/5

# INDEX

Historic county names are used throughout.
Locations without county names are in Surrey. Page numbers in **bold** indicate illustrations.